ENDORSEMENTS

Through Unity Care's success, André Chapman has proven that his innovative ideas for reforming the child welfare and foster care systems really work. Everyone who wants to do a better job of serving children, families, and communities at large should read this book and implement its comprehensive strategies!

— Roy Clay Sr.
CEO, ROD-L Electronics

An incredible story of one man's vision that is changing the lives of our society's most vulnerable population. Thanks for sharing your story. It stands as an encouragement to all!

— Marc Buller
Chief Assistant District Attorney
Santa Clara County (Retired)

As a law enforcement leader, I recognize the need to improve our foster care and educational systems, especially in our most vulnerable neighborhoods. In Roses in Concrete, *André Chapman not only points out concerns about these systems, but also offers innovative ideas about how to move forward. I applaud André for writing such an emotional and thought-provoking book! It will be abundantly clear to anyone who reads it why he is a community role model and an expert in this extremely important field.*

— Eddie Garcia
Chief of Police
San José Police Department

André Chapman has never wavered in his commitment, passion and love to make sure children in the foster care system are "seen" and treated with the utmost respect. He is a gifted leader, and relentless in never accepting anything less than the absolute best for the thousands of children he has nurtured, coached mentored over the past 25 five years. I am truly honored to call this remarkable man a dear friend, and I'm inspired by his insightful wisdom about improving systems that serve children.

— Sheila E. Mitchell
Retired Chief of Probation, Santa ClaraCounty
Chief Deputy Probation Officer Los Angeles County

ROSES IN CONCRETE

Giving Foster Children the Future They Deserve

André V. Chapman, MA

with
Michael J. Dowling

Diamond Kane Publishing
San Jose, CA

Diamond Kane Publishing
3240 S. White Road, Suite 278
San Jose, CA 95148

ISBN: 978-0-9966869-2-1   hard cover
ISBN: 978-0-9966869-0-7   soft cover
ISBN: 978-0-9966869-1-4   ebook

Cover design and interior layout by Anita Jones, Another Jones Graphics

Printed and bound in the United States of America

Publisher's Cataloging-In-Publication Data
(Prepared by The Donohue Group, Inc.)

Names: Chapman, André V. | Dowling, Michael James.
Title: Roses in concrete : giving foster care children the future they deserve / André V.
    Chapman, MA, with Michael J. Dowling.
Description: San Jose, CA : Diamond Kane Publishing, [2018]
Identifiers: ISBN 9780996686921 (hardcover) | ISBN 9780996686907 (softcover) | ISBN
    9780996686914 (ebook)
Subjects: LCSH: Foster children--Services for--United States. | Foster home care--United
    States. | Chapman, André V.--Career in social service.
Classification: LCC HV881 .C43 2018 (print) | LCC HV881 (ebook) | DDC 362.7330973--dc23

Printed in the USA

DEDICATION

We all stand on the shoulders of our ancestors, and I would like to dedicate this book to two women who have powerfully influenced my life: my grandmother and my mother.

My grandmother, Shirley Mae Chapman, was born in 1920, and today she is still as sharp as a pencil. We refer to her as Monk. She's seen a lot in her ninety-eight years, including the Jim Crow era and the Civil Rights Movement. I speak with her every Monday before I begin my week to get my critical dose of inspiration, wisdom, and historical perspective.

You'll learn something about my mom in the pages of this book, but that's just the beginning. I could go on for days relating how her work ethic, faith, integrity, love, patience, and perseverance helped lay the foundation for my life. In a very real sense, Mommy has been a grandmother to so many youths and a pillar in her community. Even today, some fifty years later, she's still teaching in the Ravenswood School District sharing her wisdom and life experiences with students.

I thank God every day for these two strong women, while painfully aware that the majority of youths in foster care have no Monk or Mom in their life.

"We make a living out of what we get, but a life out of what we give."

—Winston Churchill

TABLE OF CONTENTS

ACKNOWLEDGMENTS

It's not easy being transparent about one's life and sharing views that may be unpopular. But as Dr. Martin Luther King, Jr. so eloquently stated, "The ultimate measure of a man is not where he stands in moments of comfort and convenience, but where he stands at times of challenge and controversy."

For many years, colleagues have encouraged me to tell my story about how I left a successful career in high-tech sales to dedicate my life to serving youths in foster care. It had always been simply an interesting dinner party conversation, until at one of those dinner parties I had the privilege of meeting Juana Bordas, author of *Salsa, Soul and Spirit*. When she heard my story, she immediately asked me when I was going to finish writing my book. That conversation helped to crystalize my vision and give me the motivation I needed to begin this writing journey.

My sincere appreciation goes out to Michael J. Dowling, my professional ghostwriter and publishing guide. Like a classical pianist, he skillfully transformed my passions, convictions, and lived experiences into written words. Michael pushed me when I needed pushing, pulled back when I needed space, and prayed with me when I needed support. And of utmost significance to me, by opening their home and providing unconditional love to three beautiful adopted children, he and his wife have actually lived an important aspect of the vision I have advocated in these pages.

I also want to thank some of my close friends and colleagues who made valuable contributions to this book. They include Kathy Linton, Elizabeth Pappy, Lisa Sobrato Sonsini, Carl Agers, David Hershfield, Nancy Pena, Sheila Mitchell, Mark Yolton, Ed Walker, Walter Wilson, Deborah Tinsley, Mike Stipe, Theresa Wilson, Dyan Chan, and Cedric Martin.

I am pleased to have this opportunity to acknowledge my lovely wife, Teresa. She is my joy each morning when I awake and each evening when I lay down to sleep. She is best described by the verse in Proverbs 31:12: "She brings him good, not harm, all the days of her life." Teresa has endured the trials and tribulations at my side during the creation of this book. When I wanted to quit, she encouraged me to persevere; when I needed wise counsel, she was always there.

Finally, I want to acknowledge the other supportive members of my family. In addition to providing daily inspiration and support, they affirmed my desire to be transparent about some tough times I experienced while growing up. My foster sister, Laurel, gave me my first encounter with foster care and has made vital contributions to Unity Care. I also want to acknowledge my sister Klesha, my brother Clifford, my sister-in-law Jetrenne, my mother Shirley, and my father Clifford Jr.

x

FOREWORD

After earning All-American honors as a defensive back at the University of Southern California, Ronnie Lott played fourteen highly successful seasons in the National Football League, earning four Super Bowl rings and All-Pro honors eight times. In 2000, he was inducted into the NFL Hall of Fame. Today Mr. Lott is a successful businessman, community activist, philanthropist, and founder and executive director of All Stars Helping Kids, a non-profit organization that seeds innovative solutions to help break the cycle of poverty for Bay Area youth.

It was my good fortune to be introduced to André Chapman back around 2000 by a mutual friend, Roy Clay. At that time, André was in the midst of launching Unity Care, the extraordinary foster care ministry described in this book. He wanted to learn more about what I was doing with All Stars Helping Kids, the non-profit I had started ten years earlier to serve disadvantaged kids in the San Francisco Bay Area.

André impressed me from the first moment I met him. Although he was relatively young at the time, he was mature enough to know that life wasn't just about him. A lot of people wake up every day with the feeling that they need to do something to help other people, but they never follow through. André could have been a high-level executive with Apple, Hewlett Packard (HP), Google, or any other top-notch company. But he left a very successful career in high-tech sales because he realized that kind of success wasn't the core of who he was.

I immediately resonated with André's vision for helping at-risk kids. He believed, as I do, that with proper support, even the most disadvantaged youths can still prosper and create value for themselves. We shared a passion for helping kids arrive at the moment of realization when they can say, "Yes! I can make it. I can do this. I can go to college. I can be of value in my community. I can make my life count!"

When I was active as a professional athlete, I understood that I was ultimately working for the fans. If I did a good enough job, they eventually would notice my work. It's similar in the non-profit world. We are working for our constituency, and we constantly have to find ways to earn their respect. Respect is never simply given; it must be earned.

André has earned an enormous amount of respect. People admire him because he elevates the less fortunate. He allows them to stand on his shoulders. Stories about how he has fought for those who can't fight for themselves echo throughout our community and beyond. In a very real sense, he's not unlike Martin Luther King, Jr., Malcolm X, Jackie Robinson, Jim Brown, Tommy Mitchell, Bill Russell, Mohammed Ali, and others who laid the groundwork for those who have followed. By standing up, André is ultimately making it possible for kids to stand up.

In sports, the coaches teach you to excel and persevere. Your goal as a competitive athlete is to go out and win, not just for yourself and your team, but also for everyone in the stands. In life, kids very seldom hear this. This is especially true of kids in disadvantaged neighborhoods. Few adults care enough about them to encourage them to excel and persevere, and practically no one tells them to go out and win for "everyone."

That's what André is trying to teach youth. He's constantly challenging them to think beyond themselves and to win for "everyone." One of the things I admire most about André is that he's constantly caring for the needs of others. In those quiet moments when nobody else seems to be caring—which is precisely when caring is most needed—he is there for people.

This book is an inspiring story of vision, courage, dedication, faith, and perseverance. But more than that, it's an insightful critique of some of the serious problems that plague our current foster care and educational systems, with practical recommendations for fixing them.

André is on a mission to help rescue children and families entrapped in our dysfunctional foster care system. Having built an incredible platform in Unity Care, he is inviting others to join him in this noble cause. If we ignore his invitation, a lot of kids are going to be left behind. If we accept his challenge, a lot of lives could be transformed. One of them could be yours!

Ronnie Lott

PREFACE

The field of foster care is blessed with some of the most committed, passionate and talented professionals around. The social workers, managers, directors, case workers, courts, attorneys, and dedicated servants who staff and lead organizations at the community, county, state, and federal levels do their utmost day after day to promote the welfare of the children and youth entrusted to their care. Unfortunately, they're fighting an uphill battle, because the system is broken.

We need to think differently about how to fix the foster care system, and I'm on a mission to help do that. I hope this book will be an important tool for executing that vision. It contains field-tested ideas for setting up foster care programs that successfully transform lives. It suggests ways to improve the laws and regulations governing foster care, so they will better promote the restoration of children and families instead of contributing to their disruption. It unmasks some of the often-subtle forms of racial discrimination and biases that still exist, so we can do a better job of leveling the playing field for people of color in our society.

In these pages, I also offer some concrete recommendations for improving our educational system. My interest in education naturally evolved from my commitment to foster care. Education is key to opening the door to a hopeful future for children who are in foster care, and it is key to preventing children from entering the foster care system in the first place.

Our educational system is failing our kids, especially our children of color. In this book, I will tell you about some innovative approaches Unity Care has introduced on a pilot-project basis, with amazing results. I am hopeful that many of the changes we have pioneered will serve as models for educational and foster care reform across the United States.

This book is organized around my personal story and the story of Unity Care, the organization I founded twenty-five years ago and now lead to serve children in foster care. I chose this autobiographical format not to set myself up as an example to follow, but because I think it's the best structure for highlighting some of the personal and cultural biases that persist in our culture, some of the weaknesses of our current foster care and educational systems, and some of my ideas for practical reform. Of course, I would be thrilled if my personal story also inspires you and others to step farther out of your comfort zones and experience the joy and fulfillment of making even greater positive contributions to the lives of others.

André V. Chapman
San Jose, California

*"The world will not be destroyed by those who do evil,
but by those who watch them without doing anything."*

— Albert Einstein

CHAPTER 1

LOST LUGGAGE

As I looked out from my seat on the dais at the filled-to-capacity grand ballroom of the prestigious San Jose Fairmont Hotel, I was overwhelmed with gratitude. Around the scores of circular banquet tables in front of me were seated more than 350 citizens and community leaders who had come together to celebrate twenty years of service by Unity Care, the organization I had founded in 1993 to promote better foster care in the San Francisco Bay area.

This black-tie "YouthLive!" gala promised to be both entertaining and uplifting. In addition to hearing inspiring speeches, we would be witnessing the remarkable talents of some of the youths in our program as performers, artists, and fashion designers. Our logo for the event was the mythical Sankofa bird of West Africa. Its forward-facing body and backward-looking head perfectly expressed our goal for the evening. We wanted to glance back at the road we'd traveled, so we could more clearly see the road ahead.

The Sankofa Bird
Sankofa is an African word from the Akan tribe in Ghana. The literal translation of the word and the symbol is, "It is not taboo to fetch what is at risk of being left behind."

In my speech, I planned to acknowledge that the prior twenty years had not been easy. More than once we had wondered if we would have the funds to survive to the next day. The journey had been made more difficult by bureaucratic systems and antiquated laws, which hurt foster children more than they help them.

But I was confident that God had called me to this endeavor, and over the years He had always faithfully, and sometimes miraculously, provided for our needs. Among the faces in the audience, I recognized many that belonged to youths and families who had been part of our programs. We had made an effort to locate these graduates and get them back for this special occasion. As part of looking back, we wanted to hear their stories about how Unity Care had impacted their lives. The walls of our administrative offices are covered with photos of youths enjoying summer picnics, playing basketball, working on community service projects, and participating in other fun activities. Whenever graduates of our program come back for a visit, they always look for their own photos on these walls.

How different that is from the circumstances of most children in the foster care system who drift from home to home with their belongings in plastic bags. Many have no photos or fond memories of their childhood or adolescent years.

The first speaker this evening was State Senator Jim Beall. A strong advocate for Unity Care over the years, he said many kind words and presented the organization with a commendation from the California State General Assembly.

Patrick Willis, the all-star linebacker for the San Francisco 49ers and the honorary chairman of the event, then told the audience about his life as a foster child. One set of caring foster parents had nurtured him and his two siblings from youth to adulthood. Few kids who come through foster care are so fortunate.

State Senator Jim Beall presenting Unity Care with a certificate of commendation.

Lots of people told me I was crazy to leave a successful career in high-tech software sales to enter the non-profit sector. When I resigned my position as a highly paid executive with a Silicon Valley company to go full-time with Unity Care, I left almost $1 million of stock options on the table.

When I'm asked how I found the courage to leave that kind of money and job security behind, I always answer that the fulfillment that comes from pursuing one's passion is worth whatever sacrifices are necessary. I have never regretted that decision.

The large crowd assembled for this 20th anniversary celebration was one more testimony to how God had honored my obedience to His call on my life. It was also a reminder that I was merely the pilot, and that Unity Care was truly a collective effort.

A Moving Address

After Patrick Willis finished his remarks, I introduced Makel Ali, the evening's keynote speaker. As this young African American made his way up to the podium, dressed in a suit and tie and appearing confident, I thought back to how disheartened he had looked twenty years before, when he was the fifth youth we accepted into our program.

Makel Ali (left), Patrick Willis, and the author at YouthLive!

"My name is Makel Ali, and I know what it's like to wake up in a children's shelter," he began. "It's an awful gut-wrenching feeling to wake up one day at the tender age of fourteen and realize that no one in this world seems to care if you even exist. And that was just the harsh reality facing me one summer morning in 1993, while being housed in the Santa Clara County Children's Shelter. This was not my first morning waking up in an orphanage. No, not even close. Unfortunately for me, by age fourteen I had become a seasoned veteran of sleeping on uncomfortable, worn, and tattered cots, eating at assembly-line-like feedings, and going through the revolving doors of one failed placement after another. Yes, by fourteen, 'hope' was just an empty four-letter word that seemed to live in some far-off, desolate town that no airport or bus station sold tickets to get to."

I glanced out over the sea of people seated around the banquet tables. All eyes were riveted on Makel. He continued.

"One morning while I was sitting around in the boy's barracks trying my best to get through another long and uneventful day in the shelter, I was summoned to the front desk to take a call that had come in for me. I wondered who could be on the other end of that phone. What if it was my mom calling to say she had finally broken free from her cage of addiction and selfishness and was on her way to come pick me up? Or better yet, maybe it was my dad who had gotten wind of his son's abandonment and would rather die before letting me suffer through another day of feeling unwanted.

"It was neither of these things, but it did turn out to be a day that changed my life. It was the day that André Chapman invited me to come and live at Unity Care. Over the next four years, the staff at Unity Care gave me the tools to rebuild my life one brick at a time. They helped me mortar it together on a foundation of love, respect, integrity, responsibility, and education. They taught me valuable lessons about life and how to be a man. It was a breath of fresh air for this kid who had always felt inferior because of the color of his skin."

Many of the African Americans in the audience were nodding, indicating that they personally identified with these sentiments. Makel continued.

"At Unity Care, education was the glue that held the program together. It was non-negotiable. Once when André learned that I had missed two English classes, he removed me from a football game. I can still remember his words that day as he walked onto the football field looking every bit like a disgruntled parent. He said, 'You must have thought I was joking when I said you couldn't play. You may hate me now, but one day you'll grow to appreciate what I am doing. And Makel, I'm going to get you into college, if it's the last thing that I do.' College: what a concept! Did African Americans even go to college? Not in my house. Not in my neighborhood. Where I was from, success was not determined by college units, credits, or degrees, but rather by prison sentences, bullet wounds, and drug sales. But with countless hours of mentoring, by the time I graduated from Unity Care, I was accepted into eight universities."

This remark brought forth spontaneous applause from the audience. When it had subsided, Makel resumed speaking.

"But things did not go as I had planned. Back then, Unity Care didn't offer the Independent Living Program or the Transitional Housing Program it has today to keep graduates off the street while they're attending college. So, while most other students at my college were worried about finishing term papers or choosing a fraternity, I was making life decisions about which park bench, back seat, or men's shelter I would be sleeping in that evening. After two semesters of juggling school and homelessness, I came to the painful realization that college wasn't for me, and I reluctantly dropped out.

"After several years of going from pillar to post, I began to lose hope. I was working at a dead-end job at some drab warehouse when I got a phone call.

The voice on the other end was familiar. It was André. He wanted to know if I would like to come home to Unity Care, this time as a counselor. I accepted his job offer, and I've now worked at Unity Care for six years. People often ask me, 'Why are you so successful at counseling youth?' My answer is simple: I have experienced their hurt and pain firsthand. I have walked miles in their shoes, and I have literally slept in their beds."

At this point, many in the audience were wiping away tears. Makel turned and looked directly at me.

"André, you once told me, 'You, Makel, are a winning lotto ticket, a rose in the concrete. The world gave you rotten lemons, and you managed to make some of the sweetest lemonade. You have beaten everyone who has beaten you. I am proud to call you son.'"

"When you said those words to me, André, I could not muster up a response, because it took everything within me to hold back my tears. So, I want to say this to you today: I was once a young boy who was treated like a lost piece of luggage, and you claimed me. I was once a young man who was broken by the heavy weight of the foster care system, and you fixed me. I was once an irresponsible adult, and you still believed in me. Because of you, I stand before this crowd today—a man full of hope, integrity, spirituality, and a sense of worth. Because of you, I'm a loving husband with aspirations to be a proud father and soon-to-be college graduate. André, you are the father I often dreamed about when I would lie awake as a child in the shelter. So, if you have never heard this before, let it be clear tonight: It's from the top of my head to the bottom of my feet that I say, 'Thank you! Thank you! Thank you!'"

The entire audience rose and gave Makel a standing ovation. There were no dry eyes, including mine. It was one of the most moving experiences of my life. I am relating Makel's speech not to glorify my role in his life, or even to promote Unity Care, but simply because I think his testimony is the best way to explain why I am writing this book.

There are hundreds of thousands of abandoned kids like Makel looking for mothers and fathers who will never come. The foster care system is broken, and most of those kids bounce from home to home, like lost luggage that will never be claimed. It has been my joy and honor to be a father figure to many of them, and to help provide a safe, nurturing environment for many more. I'm writing this book because I want to encourage others to join me in this noble, fulfilling, and vital cause.

CHAPTER 2

STRADDLING TWO WORLDS

I grew up in Palo Alto, California, the "Mecca of Technology," in the heart of Silicon Valley. Back then, in the 1970s, the population was 90 percent white and 2 percent African American. I was a 2-percenter in torn blue jeans, surrounded by kids in blue blazers.

A hundred feet across the freeway from Palo Alto lies East Palo Alto. The two communities are only one expressway exit apart geographically, but they are worlds apart culturally and economically. East Palo Alto is entirely populated by people of color, by which I mean blacks and Latinos. At that time, it was known to citizens of Palo Alto as a place to avoid. Later, it would become known as the murder capital of the nation.

Although we lived in Palo Alto, my mom, Shirley Chapman, taught school in East Palo Alto. With a slight change in demeanor, I could maneuver back and forth between the two worlds, sort of like a chameleon. One day I'd be with my friends in Palo Alto, whose families took weekend trips to Lake Tahoe and Pajaro Dunes, and the next day I'd be with my friends on the other side of the freeway who didn't have food in the refrigerator. I learned early on about the difference between having and not having.

My parents, Clifford Chapman and Shirley Chapman, as high school sweethearts

Mom brought home leftover food from the school lunch program, so our refrigerator was always filled with block cheese, pizza, and little half-pint cartons of milk that had gone past the expiration date. But I was never aware that we were poor until some years later, when I got to college. One day, in a class, we discussed poverty in America, and I realized that our family fit the description.

My brother, Clifford III, is two years older than me, and my sister, Klesha, is one year older. She is deaf, so she was away at the California School for the Deaf in Berkeley during the week, and home only on the weekends. My dad, Clifford, Jr., was a salesman and wasn't around much.

Mom was a physical education teacher and basketball coach. To put food on the table, she always worked more than one job. When I was in elementary school, she also played point guard for the San Francisco Warriors of the WNBA (Women's National Basketball Association), and for a while she taught self-defense classes on local TV. When I was in middle school and high school, she also refereed college basketball games and worked in a convalescent home on weekends.

Identity Challenge

Although I felt comfortable in both worlds, it was challenging going back and forth between them. In the white community, I was always in the minority racially. Until I got to middle school, I was the only black kid in my classes.

On the other side of the freeway, in the East Palo Alto African American community, I wasn't black enough. I had to

Palo Alto Times MONDAY, DEC. 15, 1969

Basketball is more than a game to Warrior girls

They take basketball seriously

San Francisco Warrior Girls – Shirley Chapman (on left) stealing the ball during a game

be very conscious of my speech to keep from getting picked on. One time a kid said to me, "You sound like a white boy. Where you from?"

Perhaps you can spot the author in this photo of his 4th grade class!

This created an identity challenge, and I began to look around for role models. Two-parent households intrigued me, but at that time the only program on television that presented a positive image of a black middle-class family was "The Jeffersons." The family of one of my African American friends in Palo Alto became an important role model. His father was the CEO of his own company. He wore nice suits and drove a Mercedes. His mom stayed at home and didn't have to work.

The dads of several of my Palo Alto friends were very successful venture capitalists and CEOs of high-tech companies in Silicon Valley. Many of these families had second and third homes and vacationed all year around. Often, they'd invite me to go on vacations with them. It was exciting to see whole families having fun together. We didn't do that at our house.

A few of these families were African American. When I was invited to their homes, I observed what they did. While the other kids were playing in the backyard or shooting pool in the garage, I'd slip away and watch the parents and listen to their conversations. When they asked me about my parents, I'd say they were at work, which was always true about my mom. I usually didn't know where my dad was.

Watching these families taught me that education is a key to success in life. Since my mom was a school teacher, she also drummed this into me. In the earlier years when my dad was around more, he used to make my brother and me go to the library to study after school. If I disobeyed, he'd give me the belt. He was a stern disciplinarian.

After we had studied in the library for two hours, we could go next door to the recreation center, where I liked to shoot pool. One day a big kid roughed me up so he could take my place at the pool table. I rode my bike home and told my dad. He came to the center and shook that kid up a bit. Dad always taught me to stand up for myself. "Don't let anybody run you over," he would say. "You're going to face these things in life. People are going to treat you differently, and when that happens, you have to stick up for yourself."

My tenacity comes from my dad, and my compassion comes from my mom. She always talked about giving back and taking care of other people. She viewed sports as a vehicle for learning life lessons about teamwork and dealing with challenges, letdowns, goals, and controversies, so I played just about every sport growing up. That helped me stay out of trouble. The biggest enemy of kids today is unstructured time.

My parents couldn't afford to own a home in Palo Alto, but they wanted to live there instead of in East Palo Alto, so we always rented. That meant we had to move around a lot. I went to three elementary schools, one middle school, and two high schools. I didn't like this much, but it turned out to be a blessing because I got to know kids from all over.

Mom and Dad divorced when I was about ten, and I was determined not to be a burden to my mom. From that time on, I always had jobs in order to have spending money. I started out cutting grass and cleaning houses. When I turned sixteen, I got a job at Burger King and continued working there all the way through high school.

Color Bind

I noticed early on that people judged me by the color of my skin. Once the librarian at the Stanford Library asked me where I lived. When I answered "Palo Alto," she said, "Oh, you must mean East Palo Alto." My mom got really upset about that. There was just an assumption growing up that if you're black, you're from East Palo Alto.

It was always an issue to be a minority and not have the privilege and access that the white kids had. For instance, one day in the second grade, several of us were making tie-dye shirts at the recreation center after school. Our supervisor, who happened to be an African American woman, sent Chris Cardwell and me to Lucky's Supermarket to buy candy for the group. Chris, who was white, was my close childhood friend.

As we were leaving the store with the candy, the manager grabbed both of us and accused us of stealing it. He called my parents, but of course neither was at home. So he kept me there and threatened to call the police, but he let Chris go. After an hour or so, the woman who had been supervising us appeared at the store and explained that the kids had pooled their money and given it to us so we could buy candy for them. The store manager let me go, but instead of apologizing, he told me to never come back.

It was not uncommon for other kids to call me the "N" word. I first experienced this type of racial slur when it happened to my brother in elementary school. The other kid and my brother got into a fight, and the principal suspended my brother, but he didn't do anything to the white kid. When my father found out about this, he came to school and raised a stink, but it didn't change anything.

Prejudice extended beyond race. I recall one time when my sister and I rode our bicycles to the Baskin-Robbins store to get some ice cream. As I was signing with Klesha about what she wanted, the clerk who was serving us assumed we were both deaf. He turned to the other clerk and said, "Hey, why don't you help these dumb black kids." I responded with a few harsh words, and we left.

Occasionally we did a better job of standing up for ourselves. When a Radio Shack manager kicked my African American friend Chris Clay and me out of his store for no reason, Chris's dad came to the store and gave the manager a dressing down. The store manager's apology was remarkably contrite, perhaps because Chris's dad happened to be the vice mayor of Palo Alto.

Henry M. Gunn High School, where I went, was very affluent. There were lots of kids there from wealthy communities like Los Altos Hills. It was a whole world that most kids of color don't know exists, and the pressure caused me to create a fantasy story that I told to the other kids about what my parents did. About this time in my life, I began to notice the wealthy kids who drove really nice cars to school. I was so embarrassed by our old Dodge station wagon that I had my mom drop me off at the corner, so the other kids wouldn't see it.

Even though Gunn High was (and still is) one of the top high schools in the country, it had lots of racial tension. The year before I arrived, there had been a race riot, and they kept the different racial groups segregated. Sometimes fights still erupted between blacks and whites. Fortunately, I ran track, played football, badminton, and other sports, so I developed friendships in both racial groups. Sports earned me a certain amount of respect, which made high school a good experience for me, in spite of the discrimination.

Still, the prejudice was always there in some form or other. When I was fifteen and not yet old enough to have a driver's license, I would borrow my brother's license. A cop once pulled me over, but when he saw that I lived in Palo Alto, he let me go. If I had lived in East Palo Alto, I'm sure he would've arrested me. Over and over again, I saw that access often depends on things like your skin color or your zip code.

College Bound

Mom was adamant about my going to college. Since I played starting cornerback on the football team, I decided that I wanted to play football in college. I was also interested in being a police officer, so I applied to and was accepted at San Jose State University. I didn't get a football scholarship, but because I planned to major in criminology, I did get a $1,000 scholarship from the Palo Alto Police Department. That scholarship wasn't enough to pay for a dorm room, so I bunked in with my dad, who at that time lived in San Jose with his girlfriend. My goals were to play football and be a police officer.

The first goal evaporated pretty quickly. During my first semester I came down with spinal meningitis and had to spend two weeks in the hospital, where I lost thirty pounds. That ended my football career.

There was a silver lining to that cloud, however, because I now had time to join Phi Beta Sigma, a national African American fraternity. Close association with my African American fraternity brothers gave me a greater sense of what it means to be a black person in America. I became more aware of the richness of the African American legacy, which has included famous scientists, inventors, doctors, and lawyers. For example, I learned that African Americans had invented the refrigerator, the mailbox, the stoplight, and the elevator. Learning that I was descended from kings and queens of Africa boosted my confidence and self-esteem.

I also became more aware of the trauma African Americans have suffered because of racist oppression, much of it carried out through government institutions. They didn't teach this information in the Palo Alto schools when I was growing up, and most of it is not in our history books. We impoverish ourselves as a nation when we fail to adequately recognize the positive contributions of African Americans and the destructive effects of racial oppression. A greater awareness would increase empathy and understanding, which I believe would lead to inter-racial healing and spur the development of more effective policies and programs for minorities.

In my sophomore year, I moved into the fraternity house. One day I was in my second-floor room studying with my fraternity brother Alvin, when there was a knock on the door. I opened it to find two police officers standing there. One of them said, "Where is Keith Woods?"

"I don't know where he is," I answered. "He's not in my room." I knew who Keith Woods was, because he was one of my fraternity brothers, but I had no idea where he was at the time. I didn't learn until later that the police were looking for him be-

The Phi Beta Sigma fraternity house at San Jose State University

cause he had gotten into a scuffle at a campus pub. But one of the officers didn't believe I was telling the truth. "You're harboring a fugitive!" he barked, pulling out his Billy club.

Gerald, who lived in the room across the hall, heard the commotion and came over. "Hey, what's going on?"

"Get back!" one of the officers yelled at Gerald. He raised his Billy club, and it looked like he was going to strike us with it. Gerald grabbed the club, and they started tussling. The next thing I knew, Gerald had thrown the policeman's club down the stairs. That's when all hell broke loose. Both officers pounced on Alvin, Gerald, and me. They handcuffed us, dragged us down the stairs, drove us to the police station, and booked us.

This became front-page news in the campus newspaper. After a couple of weeks the police ended up dropping the charges, because we were innocent. As I recall, the school also apologized. But that incident obliterated my second goal for coming to college. Becoming a police officer no longer interested me. I switched my major from criminal justice to business administration.

CHAPTER 3

SEEING MORE CLEARLY

Working two jobs to pay my tuition on top of a lot of partying caused me to neglect my studies in my sophomore year. In order to save money, I moved into a two-bedroom apartment across town with Ron, an older fraternity brother who had finished college seven years earlier. It was great having my own place and living with someone older, but the situation started me down a road of bad decisions and wrong priorities. As time went on, I became concerned that I wasn't being true to my character.

One evening, I decided to go to a bible study with Alvin, the fraternity brother who had been with me in that police scuffle. He had asked me several times in the past to attend church with him, but I had always come up with an excuse. My grandfather, Reverend Norman Herring, was a preacher. I had grown up attending church, so I knew I was out of line by not going on a regular basis. That night, the pastor went around praying for each of us. I don't remember what he said when he prayed over me, but I fell down on my knees, asked God for forgiveness, and accepted Jesus Christ as my Lord and Savior.

That next semester, I decided to move back into the fraternity house, and my life got back on track. My fraternity, Phi Beta Sigma, emphasized community service, and when I mentioned to my mom that we were working with kids at a San Jose high school, she asked if we would be willing to do something for the kids at her school in East Palo Alto.

Over the next few weeks, some of my fraternity brothers and I developed a mentoring program. This involved bringing a group of ten high school boys to San Jose State one Friday through Sunday to get a taste of college life. Just living in the fraternity house and attending classes with us was so motivating for these kids! We'd plant visions in their minds about becoming successful doctors, engineers, attorneys, CEOs, congressmen, and other professionals and leaders. As we mentored them, they got to see positive images of African American college students.

The following semester we brought the same group of ten boys back to the campus for another long weekend. Unfortunately, we found that we had to restart our mentoring from the ground level. While back in their normal environment during the intervening six months, with limited resources in the schools, crime in the neighborhoods, and few positive role models in their lives, they had reverted to their old ways of thinking. Three days twice a year just didn't allow enough time to make a lasting impact on their lives.

In spite of these limitations, however, the program was a big success, and we repeated it the following year with another group of ten kids. One of the youths from this program ended up coming to San Jose State and actually joining our fraternity.

Starting a Career

When I graduated in 1988, I moved back home with my mom, who was now living in Sunnyvale, and launched my post-college career. I really enjoyed my job as a sales representative to high-tech companies for Businessland Computers, the first billion-dollar reseller of computers. But four months into it, HR called and asked me to come to corporate headquarters. When I arrived, a lady from HR and a man from risk management ushered me into an office. "We heard you're doing a great job," the man said, "but unfortunately we have to let you go. You didn't disclose on your resume that you were once arrested."

I was devastated. It hadn't even occurred to me to disclose my arrest on my application because San Jose State had dropped all charges. But now, this unfortunate incident had come back to haunt me. I suppose if I had thought to disclose my arrest on my application, this company wouldn't have hired me anyway, even though I was innocent. I cried the whole time driving home. I couldn't get up the nerve to tell my mom what happened.

A short time later, I landed a job as a sales associate with MicroAge Computers. After a while, I moved on to Kellner Systems, a small company that sold Unix-based practice-management systems to doctors. The CEO of Kellner, Peter Kellner, was a great guy who taught me a lot about business.

Birth of a Vision

My job had me flying all over the country. On one of these flights, I happened to read an article in *Black Enterprise* magazine about a man named Kenneth Hill, who created a technical education program in Detroit called the Detroit Area Pre-College Engineering Program (DAPCEP). His goal was to give disadvantaged kids a technological career pipeline into the Big Three automotive companies.

I already had an interest in exposing minority kids to high-tech careers, and I had seen how some of my fraternity brothers had gained access to business careers through corporate internships that began while they were in college. I felt it was a shame that we were letting so much talent go to waste in Silicon Valley, the Mecca of technology. I called Kenneth Hill and asked if I could spend a day with him the next time I was in his area.

A few months later, after I had finished working with a client in Dearborn, I went to see Ken. What he showed me changed my life forever. He had created a curriculum in partnership with all of the local schools, and even some local colleges, that exposed kids in elementary school to technology and various career opportunities in the automotive industry.

He took me to General Motors to meet a manager who had graduated from his program fifteen years earlier. This manager could hardly contain his excitement as he told me how DAPCEP had sparked his interest in technology and opened the door for his current career. Ken explained how this man and many other successful graduates of DAPCEP were now investing their lives back into the underserved local communities from which they had come. By the end of the day, I realized that my passion was to expose kids to technology, but I didn't know quite how to make that happen.

A few weeks later, while I was in LA on business, I had dinner with a couple of my fraternity brothers, Delano Johnson and Darryl Cullins. When I told them both about my idea of wanting to expose kids to technology, Delano said I should see the residential treatment program where he worked. After dinner, he drove me over to a two-story Victorian home, where six boys were living in a foster care environment. It had a ping-pong table, a pool table, exercise equipment, and some other impressive stuff.

I was already exposed to foster care, because after I left home for college, my mom became a foster parent to a ten-year-old girl named Laurel, who became my little sister. But I had never talked to Laurel in depth about her background, so the next time I was home, I asked Laurel to share her personal story. After listening to my foster sister, I realized that I wanted to start a foster care residential program that focused on connecting kids to technology.

My family growing up: Laurel, Klesha, Shirley (Mommy), Clifford, and me

CHAPTER 4

JUGGLING PRIORITIES

Throughout 1990, while putting in sixty-hour workweeks for Kellner Systems, I spent my "spare time" learning about the complex foster care system. I found out that it was common for foster children to be moved in and out of twenty or more homes during their tenure in foster care. With no stability in their lives and no one to love them unconditionally, they understandably became even more traumatized, sad, discouraged, depressed, confused, and angry. I have since learned that about 27 percent of young adult prison inmates in California have experienced a foster care placement[1], and about 70 percent of all San Quentin Prison inmates at any one time are products of the foster care system![2]

At the Santa Clara County children's shelter, I was shocked to see the overcrowded conditions. Kids were shuffled around like cattle, and at that time due to overcrowding, some even slept on mattresses on the floors. The majority of them were African American and Latino. Even though African Americans comprised only 3 percent and Latinos only 30 percent of the county's population, they made up 13 percent and 62 percent of the county's foster care population, respectively.

The more I studied the situation, the more committed I became to my vision. I began putting together a business proposal for a 501(c)3 non-profit corporation that would provide residential foster care treatment services for boys. My desire was to offer a positive living environment, with emphasis on exposing kids to the world of technology. I chose the name "Unity Care Group" because I wanted my staff and our supporters to work as a group in *unity* to provide *care* for foster children, with the ultimate goal of *uniting* them with *caring* families. My CEO, Peter Kellner, supported my idea, even though he had recently given me additional responsibilities by promoting me to National Director of Sales.

At the time, there were approximately 100,000 kids in California's foster care system. I learned later that about one-fourth were being treated with psy-

[1] http://www.cdss.ca.gov/cdssweb/entres/pdf/CaliforniaStatePrison-ChildWelfareDataLinkage-Study.pdf

[2] http://earlypoint.com/2006/08/staggering-statistics-about-us-foster.html

chotropic drugs. A large portion of these drugs were psychotropic medications, which are intended for only the most serious mental issues, such as schizo-phrenia and bipolar disorders. Because these drugs are highly profitable, some pharmaceutical companies aggressively promote them for treating foster care children. In the short term, psychotropic medications tend to transform kids into zombies; in recent years, it's been reported that long-term use can cause tremors, diabetes, and other serious health problems.[3]

My next step was to form a board of directors. I started with two men who had served as my mentors growing up. One was Roy Clay, who was the first product manager at Hewlett-Packard and the first African American vice mayor of Palo Alto. Roy was the father of one of my best friends, Chris Clay, who also later joined the board. Another mentor who accepted my invitation to join the board was a successful Palo Alto businessman and former professional foot-ball player, Henry Ford. His son, Mark Ford, was my brother Cliff's best friend when they were younger. Even though Henry was unrelated to the automobile magnate, Pittsburgh Steelers fans had given him the moniker "Model T."

During this two-year planning period, I also purchased my first home, a three-bedroom, two-bathroom place in a suburb community of San Jose. I was determined not to repeat the experiences I had growing up, when our family was constantly moving from one rental home to another. I rented out the other two rooms to my fraternity brothers, and we all moved in.

Preparing

In early 1992, I began hunting for a home that I could rent to serve as our resi-dential foster home, but landlords didn't seem to want a house full of foster kids in their neighborhood. After nearly a year with no success, I came up with the idea of turning my personal home into a residential foster care home. My college sweetheart, Charlene, moved in with me. We were engaged to be married, and she was pregnant with our first child. Although she wasn't keen on the idea of having to move while pregnant, she agreed with my vision and said okay.

Quite a number of my work friends, family members, and fraternity brothers thought I was crazy. One of my fraternity brothers—his name was Ed Walker, but we called him "Smiley"—said, "Man, what do you mean you're going to move out of your home? Are you crazy?!"

Smiley wasn't the only fraternity brother who thought I was crazy, but over time many of them ended up resonating with my vision. When I opened the home, quite a few signed up to work as full-time and part-time paid staff. My

---

[3] These drugs are still widely used today. For more information on this subject, see "Drugging Our Kids," published in the August 14, 2014, issue of the *San Jose Mercury News*. It can be read online at http://webspecial.mercurynews.com/druggedkids/

mom put together educational lesson plans, and some friends agreed to serve on the board. These people were a great support to me while I was developing the plans for this home.

The residential facility had to pass a state inspection before we could officially open it. This meant that it had to have three identical bedrooms, each furnished with two beds, and it had to have an office, which I intended to make by converting the living room. On the day of the inspection, the home had to be completely ready, as if it were going to open for business the very next day.

Since I didn't have any money to transform our house into a residential facility, I went to see one of our board members, Mr. Perry Taylor, an African American businessman who lived in San Jose and worked as a technician for Pacific Bell Telephone Company. He graciously agreed to loan me $20,000.

On August 31, 1992, after much work, the house was ready for inspection. I submitted the application to the state, and on October 15, we received notice that our inspection would take place in seven days.

Charlene and I had already put most of our belongings in storage, and we were living in the house out of suitcases and boxes containing only our bare necessities. On the day before the inspection, I packed these necessities into our car and parked it in an inconspicuous place around the corner. Although seven months pregnant, Charlene endured this "forced evacuation" like a trooper.

House #1 – Our first residential treatment home

I spent the week prior to the inspection making sure everything in the house was perfect. Finally, the big day arrived. I did one final run-through and anxiously waited for the inspector to appear. Then, moments before the inspector was due to arrive, the house's water heater broke! In a panic, I called Mr. Taylor, who could fix just about anything. Fortunately, I caught him at home, and he came right over.

When the inspector arrived, Mr. Taylor was on the floor, surrounded by plumbing tools and an array of parts from the disassembled water heater. "It's just broken," I nervously explained. "We'll have it fixed in no time."

As I escorted the inspector through the other rooms in the house, my mind was on that water heater. If Mr. Taylor didn't fix it quickly, we could flunk the inspection. That could mean the death of my vision before it truly started.

Fortunately, Mr. Taylor had the water heater fixed and put back together by the time we returned. As the inspector left, she seemed to be in a positive mood. I retrieved our car from its clandestine parking place, and Charlene and I moved back into the house.

Waiting

We also moved into a waiting phase. We waited for Charlene's pregnancy to come to term, and we waited for the State of California to tell us whether we had passed the inspection. That first wait was rewarded on January 11, 1993, when Charlene gave birth to our first son, André Valísque, Jr. The second was rewarded on April 16, 1993, when we received a license from the state that permitted us to operate a residential home for foster children.

This second bit of good news was less exciting than it might have been, however, because California was in the midst of a budget crisis. The state legislature had been unable to pass a budget that the governor was willing to sign, and all funding was on hold. Without state funding, we couldn't operate the house, so it made no sense to open it.

Charlene and I took advantage of this lull to celebrate a June wedding and enjoy a seven-day honeymoon in Jamaica. Finally, in July, the state passed a budget, and I received our official funding letter. We were now in a position to open our foster care home. This meant that Charlene and I had to find another place to live, so I again called Mr. Taylor. In addition to working for Pacific Bell, he invested in real estate and owned a number of rental properties. He agreed to rent one of these to us, and we moved into it in late July.

On August 14, while I was attending a sales conference in Fort Myers, Florida, I received a call from the Santa Clara County Department of Social Services asking me to come and pick up our first foster child. That was impossible for me to do personally from the other side of the country, so I called Cedric Martin, who at this time was employed by State Farm Insurance in San Jose. Cedric and I had lived in the fraternity house together and had graduated from college the same year. He was one of our first part-time staff who supported my idea of opening the home. "Hey, Cedric, I need you to do me a favor. We received a call to come and get our first youth. Can you go down and pick him up and then stay with him for the weekend?"

"No problem," Cedric answered. When I got back in town, I thanked Cedric profusely, and we started our program in earnest. Some years later, Cedric became a member of Unity Care's board of directors.

Almost immediately, we were flooded with phone calls from social workers who were eager to place kids. Because we were the new program on the block, we were asked to take the most difficult cases, the ones nobody else wanted to accept. Most of these kids had been in ten to fifteen prior placements each, which typically meant they had lived in that many different neighborhoods and gone to as many different schools. We readily accepted them, however, because we believed that every child deserves a chance.

Serving

Even though we had the most difficult population of kids, our program was extremely successful, largely because of our unique setup. About seven fraternity brothers worked as full-time and part-time paid staff in our house, caring for six boys. One served as facility manager and worked weekdays from 7:00 a.m. to 3:00 p.m., two worked the evening shift from 3:00 p.m. to 11:00 p.m., and one worked the graveyard shift from 11:00 p.m. to 7:00 a.m. Different staff came in on the weekends.

The staff cooked the meals, and the kids learned by assisting them. Since all staff members were college students, education was a constant topic of conversation. Occasionally, the staff would take the boys to the university library for study hour. This was an inspiring experience for the kids, since most had never dreamed of going to college. In fact, most had never even known anyone who had gone to college.

Because my fraternity brothers were African American and looked like the majority of the population we served, strong bonds developed between them. The boys looked up to the staff as role models and big brothers. The fraternity brothers who played college football especially motivated the youths who played or aspired to play sports.

We maintained a consistent routine. During the week, the staff member on the graveyard shift cooked breakfast and got the kids off to school. The facility manager looked over things during the day, checked on the boys at school, and occasionally met with county social workers. Workers on the evening shift supervised the study time, which was from 3:00 p.m. to 5:00 p.m. on weekday afternoons, and served dinner at 7:00 p.m. In the evenings, my foster sister, Laurel, who was then a student at San Jose State, offered tutoring sessions for the boys. As time went on, she enlisted the help of some of her girlfriends as tutors and additional counselors. In addition to helping the kids with academics and personal issues, they provided a big sister/motherly influence.

Activities and outings were a huge part of our program. On Saturdays, we went on field trips and did fun activities. One week we might go to the circus, to the beach, or even to Lake Tahoe. The next week we might go horseback riding or to an amusement park or to a college basketball or football game.

Everyone went to church on Sunday mornings. Then we'd go to a restaurant for Sunday dinner, or we might go to my mom's house to enjoy one of her fabulous home-cooked meals. Sunday afternoons were free time, when kids could visit families, or families could come to the house to visit the kids. This

University of Southern California (USC) college tour – Summer of Learning

positive, family-like environment was very successful in building trust. We had so much success, in fact, that in early 1994, the county urged us to open another home.

"Let's repeat the process we used with our first home," I suggested to Charlene. "We can turn the house we're living in into a residential facility." The Stipes, who were our good friends and godparents to André Jr., lived close by and had plenty of space. We agreed that Charlene and André Jr. would move in with them temporarily, and that I would prepare our current house for the state inspection, while living in it with our dog, Ebony. This was emotionally tough, but I promised Charlene I would find a home for us before she gave birth to our second child.

Racing

The county was so eager for us to open our next home that we had a wait list of youth referred to our program before we opened our doors. In fact, we opened house #2 before I had time to find a permanent home for my family, so we continued to live with the Stipes.

On December 18, 1994, four months after opening house #2, I got a call at work from Charlene, who at this time was nine months pregnant. "My water has broken!" she exclaimed.

Fortunately, Mike Stipe happened to be home at the time. He rushed Charlene to the hospital, and I met them there. A short time later, she gave birth to a healthy baby boy, whom we named Aaron Vincent.

The doctors told me that Charlene had to remain in the hospital for a few days to heal from her procedure. This gave me much-needed extra time to finalize the deal on a home I had picked out. We signed the closing documents in the hospital, just before Charlene was discharged. By God's grace, I was able to keep my promise to her that we would have a new home by the time she was discharged from the hospital.

The hectic pace continued. My job as National Director of Sales for Kellner Systems typically kept me away from home one to two weeks per month. Whenever I came back to San Jose, I'd drop by the two residential homes and make sure things were running smoothly. Often, I'd come to the homes around 10 p.m., talk with the youth, sleep in the back office, and leave early the next morning. On Sunday evenings, Charlene would cook a big dinner, and I would have the facility managers over to review the progress of every youth and handle various operational matters. My foster sister, Laurel, would serve as our administrative secretary at these meetings.

Although I very much enjoyed my work and greatly admired my boss, after nearly six years of constant traveling, the job at Kellner Systems was wearing me down. So, I accepted a sales position with a local technology company called Net-Manage. This job required no travel, which meant that I could devote more time to my family and Unity Care.

The more relaxed pace was a welcome change, but within about twelve months, a really interesting opportunity came my way. Aironet Wireless Communications, a fast-growing wholly-owned subsidiary of Telxon Corporation, asked me to join them as their Director of Sales for their West Coast operations. I hesitated about taking this new position, which required a time commitment of about sixty hours a week. Even though Charlene was pregnant again, the upside potential seemed too good to pass up. The company was poised to go public, and my incentive package included 10,000 shares of pre-IPO stock.

Joining Aironet in March 1996 put my life in hyperspeed again. The company was a major contributor to the 802.11 standards for wireless communications and a leading provider of high-speed wireless network connectivity. We were in the middle of the dot-com boom, the economy was roaring, and Aironet was growing like wildfire. As the person in charge of sales for the western region, I was at the epicenter of the action. I was working with a great group of guys, and I was excited about the technology we were selling. Things couldn't have been better.

Then, out of the blue, the executive vice president and chief operating officer — the man who had hired me and with whom I worked very closely — was let go. The vice president of OEM sales became the chief operating officer, and he wasted no time in raising the bar. He was under tremendous pressure to bring in more business, and he passed that pressure down to me. Instantly, I felt like I had been pulled out of a refreshing swimming pool and tossed in an overheated Jacuzzi.

Meanwhile, Unity Care kept growing. When the county saw that this second home was also successful, and that we had a long waiting list of children wanting to get in, they asked us to expand again. So, on July 15, 1996, we opened house #3.

One day in November, while I was in the middle of a sales appointment, I got a call from Charlene. "I'm heading for the hospital," she said. "You need to get there quick."

I called my boss to tell him what was happening. I sort of expected him to say something like, "Congratulations! Go be with your wife and let me know if you need to take some time off." But instead he said, "Call me back later today so we can review your sales funnel report."

When I arrived at the hospital, the nurses were waiting for me. They threw me into a wheelchair and rolled me into the operating room. Fifteen minutes later, at 2:58 p.m. on November 3, 1996, our daughter, Ariana Vanessa, was born. After my mom and mother-in-law arrived at the hospital and things had calmed down, I went back to my office. My boss had some hard deadlines and didn't seem to care one whit about what was happening with my family. All he cared about was my report and the sales numbers. That was a turning point for me. I knew I couldn't continue to work in such an intense, hard-driving, and at times insensitive environment.

Over the next several months, the mounting pressures at work made it extremely difficult to honor my increasing responsibilities as a husband and a father of three little ones. I was being crushed under the weight of all the pressure, because my commitments to Unity Care left me little time and energy to spare. One day my boss showed up from back east to discuss my performance, and we agreed to part ways.

CHAPTER 5

REORDERING PRIORITIES

In retrospect, I realized I hadn't been giving 100 percent to my job with Aironet. My primary passions were Unity Care and my family. Both desperately needed my attention, and it was hard to devote adequate time and energy also to my job.

Most business professionals hate being unemployed, but I was okay with it. For the first time since starting Unity Care, I had time to breathe. I relished spending more time with my family and at the residential homes, and it occurred to me that I should consider going full-time with Unity Care. But I doubted that a fledgling non-profit could support our family, so I quickly squelched that idea. Working full-time with foster children was never my intent.

During this time, I had been receiving calls about different job opportunities. Wendell Uddyback, a former colleague at NetManage, connected me with the CEO of Resource One Computer Systems. The company was based on the East Coast, and he was looking for a general manager on the West Coast. In June 1997, I accepted his offer.

This job was similar to my previous one, only better. My office was in San Jose, and for the first time in about six years, I was not required to travel. I could now be home in the evenings with my family and have more time for Unity Care. After experiencing so much stress for so long, it felt great to slow down.

One day, Laurel and a couple of other members of our female staff approached me about opening a home for girls. Initially, I balked. Up to that point we had only cared for boys. But the women felt strongly about it, homes for girls were a pressing need, and so on February 10, 1998, we opened house #4 to accommodate six girls. Unity Care now had a staff of about thirty-five counselors, tutors, and social workers who were caring for twenty-four kids.

We were barely making a dent in the needs we saw all around us, so I decided to turn the home Charlene and I were living in into Unity Care house #5, using the same "cookie cutter" approach we had used with houses #1 and #2. This time, however, we didn't have to first pack our belongings into boxes and move out. Thanks to the strong economy and the substantial bonuses that I had been earning with my technology job, we had enough resources to build ourselves a nice home in suburban San Jose.

In May 1999, Charlene and I and the kids moved into our new home, and Unity Care opened the doors of house #5. This brought Unity Care's population to thirty foster kids and almost fifty full-time and part-time staff. Things seemed to be going well. Our program was positively impacting the lives of youths: the county was pleased, staff members were excited, and I believed I was doing exactly what I had been created to do.

Aaron Vincent (left), Ariana Vanessa, and André Valísque

I should have felt fulfilled and happy, but I did not. The pressures of trying to juggle three huge responsibilities— family, job, and Unity Care— were tearing me apart. I kept seeing opportunities for Unity Care to expand its ministry, which I didn't have time to pursue. For example, we had developed a very successful violence prevention program for our foster kids. A school system heard about it and offered us quite a bit of money to offer it in schools, but I was forced to turn them down because of time constraints.

Another problem was that quite a few kids who graduated from our program ended up homeless, but I didn't have the time and resources to develop the follow-up programs necessary to help them. This need wasn't unique to Unity Care. Nationwide, most of the 20,000 young people who annually age out of foster care must head out into the world with no family, no money, and no support. The majority are able to carry all of their worldly possessions in a few plastic bags.

Approximately half of those who start high school end up dropping out. Only a few make it to college, and most of those don't finish. A study at the University of Chicago of former foster children in the Midwest found that only 2.5 percent had graduated from college by age twenty-six.[4] These were just a few of the unmet needs that surfaced as we worked with these kids and their families. It was frustrating because we always felt the children deserved better.

One Sunday, as I was sitting in church worrying about how to deal with the conflicting pulls in my life, the pastor preached a sermon that seemed meant just for me. I don't remember the exact scripture he referenced— perhaps it was Proverbs 3:5-6, which says, "Trust in the Lord with all your heart, and lean not on your own understanding. In all your ways acknowledge him, and he will direct

[4] http://www.chapinhall.org/sites/default/files/Midwest%20Evaluation_Report_4_10_12.pdf

your paths." Or maybe it was Jesus' admonition in Matthew 6:24: "No one can serve two masters, for either he will hate the one and love the other, or he will be devoted to the one and despise the other. You cannot serve God and money."

Although I don't remember the exact scriptures, I will never forget something else about that sermon. At one point, Pastor Jones seemed to look straight at me and ask, "Are you walking in faith, or are you walking in the ways of the world?" Interestingly, these very thoughts had been circulating in my mind for several weeks, but I had suppressed them. Now God seemed to be forcing the issue. Right there in the service I made a commitment to God that I would leave my job and trust in Him to provide.

Keeping My Commitment

Making that commitment was easier than keeping it, however. Even though I knew that my lack of passion limited my upward potential in high-tech, the pull of stock options and other monetary benefits was strong. There's a reason why people in the industry call these types of incentives "golden handcuffs."

At that time, we were in the early days of the dot-com boom, and companies were going public and getting bought out left and right. Scores of people who worked for these Silicon Valley companies were becoming millionaires overnight. In fact, Cisco Systems had recently purchased Aironet Wireless Communications for about $90 per share. If I had stayed with the company, my 10,000 shares would have been worth about $900,000. I left that kind of money on the table once. Did I want to do that again by resigning from a flourishing high-tech startup that was positioning itself to go public?

When I called my mom and told her about what had happened to me in church, she advised me to do whatever God led me to do. As was her custom, she shared a Bible verse with me. On this occasion, it was about being prayerful and listening to God. But still, I hesitated. Money is a powerful force if you are serving two masters. A week went by and then a month. Before long, I was as busy as ever.

About this time, one of our largest mainframe clients made a critical decision to change vendors. This customer was responsible for about 50 percent of our unit's business, so I wasn't surprised when the CEO called me at the end of the month and told me that the company was closing its Silicon Valley office. He told me to spend the next month winding down our operations.

If I had received this call a month earlier, before I had the encounter with the Lord in the church service, I probably would have operated on cruise control and simply looked for another job in San Jose. I was constantly getting calls from companies who wanted me to come to work for them, so finding a new position would have been rather easy. But because God had spoken to me, I took this as confirmation that He wanted me to stop chasing the money and focus on Unity Care.

After I left Resource One Computer Systems, I met with my staff and board of directors and informed them that I would be devoting 100 percent of my time to Unity Care. Although my mouth uttered these words with some enthusiasm, my mind was battling uncertainty. I had grown quite addicted to the stock options, bonuses, and other financial incentives that come with a Silicon Valley high-tech career, and I wondered how long I could resist the temptation to bounce back in.

Fortunately, Charlene had gone back to school to become a surgical technician and was bringing in some extra income from her part-time job with the county. But that wasn't enough to support our family, and I was nervous about the financial risks associated with this change of career.

After I went full-time with Unity Care, the organization really began to evolve. We opened an administrative office, and our programs expanded. I operated the ministry like a startup business, with a very entrepreneurial culture. For instance, when I asked my staff if any of them had experience with hiring, one person said she had been a manager with a Gap clothing store, so I made her our HR director. I learned that our FedEx delivery guy worked on computers after hours, so I hired him to be our part-time IT manager.

As my vision for the organization enlarged, so did my expectations for the staff. But managing a social service, non-profit environment turned out to be very different from running a profit-driven business. The bottom line, performance-based orientation I had inherited from the private sector clashed with Unity Care's more laid back, non-profit culture, and I came down too hard on some of my staff. Fortunately, my leadership style and the organization's culture both changed, and we continued to prosper.

Growing

Over the next few months, we added several new community-based programs and even some mental health initiatives. Dr. Glen Toney, senior VP of Applied Materials, a very successful Silicon Valley company, and Mr. Jim Morgan, the company's CEO, spearheaded a $50,000 grant from their corporation. We used this as seed money to launch an engineering program in June of 1999 that had been high on my to-do list for a long time. We called it the Pre-College Minority Engineering Program (PC-MEP). It was modeled after the Detroit Area Pre-College Engineering Program (DAPCEP) that had so impressed me some years earlier.

PC-MEP was an eight-week intensive summer program that brought students to San Jose State University and exposed them to science, math, technology, and engineering. A high school teacher and a college professor taught the curriculum, which was focused on math and science. Every Tuesday, an engineer or a technology person from a high-tech company would come to San Jose State and educate the students about their company, its products, and their job. The students would spend the following day at that technology company, getting hands-on application experience.

A weekly visit of PC-MEP to Applied Materials, Inc.

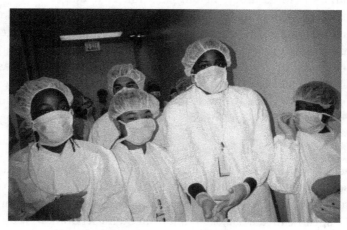

A PC-MEP visit to Seagate Technology

We offered the PC-MEP opportunity to youths in the community as well, so about 100 students became involved. We also developed a youth robotics program that attracted about thirty students during the regular school year. One of the big buzzwords in educational circles today is "STEM," which is an acronym for "science, technology, engineering, and mathematics." We were doing STEM before STEM became fashionable.

The time seemed ripe to launch another initiative that had been in my heart since 1997. I became aware of the need when I witnessed what happened when

Makel Ali graduated after many years in our program. As you may recall from Chapter 1, Makel was the keynote speaker at Unity Care's 2013 YouthLive! event. Upon graduation, Makel had football opportunities at a number of first-rate colleges. He chose to attend San Jose State, but a year after he enrolled, he had to withdraw because he didn't have enough money to pay for a dorm room. For a while, he tried to live in his car, but that didn't work. Eventually, he dropped out of school and entered the ranks of the homeless.

I shared Makel's story with Jim Beall, who today is a state senator, but at that time was on the local Board of Supervisors. I said, "Jim, we removed these kids from their homes with the promise that we will give them a better life. We put them in foster care where they are often moved from home to home and school to school, with a considerable amount of abuse and neglect along the way. Then, at age eighteen, we turn them out on the street to fend for themselves. That's horrific!"

For the next year, Supervisor Beall helped us lobby the Social Services Agency (SSA) to develop a plan to address the huge need for homeless youths who had aged out of foster care. In late 1999, SSA finally awarded us a three-year grant, and in December of that year we opened house #6. Its sole purpose was to provide transitional housing and support for youths aging out of foster care. As far as I know, this program was one of the first in Northern California to specifically address this transitional housing need for former foster youths who were homeless.

A Divine Appointment

The dot-com boom continued to heat the economy. Companies and headhunters were constantly calling to see if I would like to get back into high-tech sales. When friends told me how much money they were making, I was tempted to do it.

In early 2000, Dr. Glen Toney invited me to a private dinner with Coretta Scott King, the widow of Dr. Martin Luther King, Jr. I was excited, but also nervous about meeting this great woman and national icon. When we arrived, Glen took me over to her. "Mrs. King, I'd like to introduce you to André Chapman. He's the founder and CEO of a non-profit organization that works with foster children."

I reached out to shake Mrs. King's hand, but instead of shaking my hand, she held it tightly and pulled me closer. Then she looked directly into my eyes and said, "I sense that God is going to expand your ministry and allow you to touch thousands of children. You will have a huge impact on many lives, so trust in Him. I would like to pray for you." As she prayed over me, right there in the middle of that busy evening, it brought back memories of how my grandmother used to pray over me as a child.

Coretta Scott King praying for me

Meeting *the* Coretta Scott King was a once-in-a-lifetime experience beyond anything I could have ever imagined. Now, I had not only met her, I had been privileged to experience a remarkable, unforgettable moment with her when God truly showed up. In retrospect, I believe God used this encounter to confirm that I was on the path He had for me.

CHAPTER 6

ALL IN

About six months into my full-time commitment, I happened to be going to a San Francisco 49ers football game with Mike Stipe and Carl Agers, two buddies I had worked with at Businessland Computers back in 1988. Mike was now the VP of Sales for an exciting new startup called NonStopNet, and Carl was the company's VP of Marketing.

Hey, André," Mike said to me. "We know that your passion is Unity Care, but you need to make some money to take care of your family. Why don't you come to work for me as an inside sales rep. You won't have to travel, so you can be home with your wife and kids every night. And I will give you flexibility with your schedule, so you can still have time for Unity Care. Our goal is to take the company public or get bought out, and you should be able to get some pre-IPO stock. What do you say?"

"It's a great opportunity," Carl added. "You could come work with us for a year, and then you could go back to Unity Care with some cash."

I thought, well, this is interesting. Maybe this is God's way of allowing me to work with Unity Care and support my family at the same time. It's the best of both worlds. I promised Mike that I'd consider the idea and get back to him.

In order to make this opportunity work, I needed to find someone to manage Unity Care. I happened to know a fellow named Aubrey Merriman, who had been the executive director of a local non-profit organization. We had served together on the board of Sacred Heart Community Services, another non-profit in San Jose, and I had always been very impressed with him.

Although Aubrey was currently working, I gave him a call. "Listen, Aubrey, I'm thinking about going back into high-tech sales, and I'm looking for someone to manage the day-to-day operations of Unity Care as the executive director. Are you possibly interested?"

My call took him by surprise, but he said he would like to know more. We met several times, and he seemed perfect for the job, so I made him an offer to start in two weeks. Meanwhile, after two weeks of discussions, I accepted Mike's offer to start work at NonStopNet on the following Monday, the same day Aubrey was due to start at Unity Care.

It seemed that God was working everything out perfectly! I had found the ideal guy to run Unity Care, and I had found the ideal job for allowing me to both support my family and pursue my passion of helping foster youth.

On September 22, 2000, the Saturday before Aubrey and I were to start our new jobs, I hosted my thirty-fifth birthday party at my house. I had invited Mike Stipe and Carl Agers, but halfway through the party I noticed that Mike hadn't shown up. "Where's Mike?" I asked Carl. "Oh, he had to work today," Carl answered. "Our CEO is in town, and he wanted to meet with him." That made sense, so I forgot about it.

On the following day, Sunday, I tried to reach Mike to find out what time I should report to work on Monday, but I was unable to reach him. Meanwhile, Aubrey Merriman called me. "André," he said, "I've got some bad news. I'm not going to be able to start as Executive Director of Unity Care tomorrow. I'm in the United States on a Canadian work visa, and my wife and I are concerned that the Canadian government will not adjust it to allow me to take another job in the same industry as my previous job."

"Oh, my God!" I thought. "What am I going to do? I'm supposed to start my new job at NonStopNet tomorrow, and now I don't have anyone to take my place at Unity Care." I tried again to phone Mike, but he still didn't answer. There was nothing I could do but wait until Monday morning.

Early Monday morning, I called Carl at the office. "Hey Carl, I haven't heard from Mike, and I don't know what time to come in or who I should to report to."

"Haven't you heard?" said Carl. "Mike and the company had a parting of ways."

"You must be kidding me!" I exclaimed. "What does that mean for me?"

"I suggest that you call HR and find out," Carl answered.

When I finally got in touch with the appropriate person in HR, she said, "All personnel decisions related to sales are on hold for reevaluation. At this time, we will not be moving forward with your offer."

I was dumfounded! The whole game plan I had constructed over the past month, which I thought God had orchestrated with amazing precision, had crumbled right in front of me within the span of twenty-four short hours. After I got over the initial shock, I realized that this was God's way of caring for me. He was saying, "What are you doing? You are not walking in faith. You are again trying to lean on your own understanding." Then and there I made up my mind that I would never again try to serve two masters.

Breaking Free

It had taken me six years, but I was finally beginning to focus on the long-term good, instead of merely on the short-term gain. As I witnessed the growth and increasing impact of Unity Care, I was learning firsthand how God blesses us when we trust in Him.

Not long after that, I ran into a gentleman who had given me some helpful advice a few years before, when I was doing research about whether to open my first residential home. He said he was about to retire from his position as executive director of his foster care program, and he asked me if I would be interested in absorbing the six residential houses that he operated. It seemed like a good fit, so over the next year we took over the management of these homes.

This acquisition expanded our reach beyond Santa Clara County to Santa Cruz and Monterey Counties. Within one year of committing myself full-time to Unity Care, we had grown from five foster homes to twelve, and from about 50 employees to approximately 130.

We were providing numerous community programs, including a violence-prevention program we launched in the public schools with funding from the Packard Foundation. These additional tools in our toolbox allowed us to expand our impact. The needs of the community, not the needs of our organization, drove everything we did.

To supplement the normal operating funds that we received from the state, we applied for grants and organized additional fund-raising events. One of the most successful events was the Virginia Clay Unity Care Golf Classic, which

we held annually in honor of Virginia Clay, who had passed away a few years earlier due to cancer. She was the wife of Roy Clay, Unity Care's first board member, and the mother of my childhood friend and Unity Care board member Chris Clay. Because of my previous experience in high-tech sales and Mr. Clay's long-term business relationships, we were able to recruit many technology companies as sponsors for this event.

At the third annual Virginia Clay/Unity Care Golf Classic at Silver Creek Valley Country Club in San Jose, California in 2001. From left: Roy Clay, chairman of the golf committee; the author, Ronnie Lott, NFL Hall of Fame football player; Carl Agers, Unity Care board member; the author; Mike Stipe, Unity Care board member.

At the Virginia Clay/Unity Care Golf Classic
From left: Tyrone Willingham, Stanford University head football coach; Roy Clay, CEO of ROD-L Electronics; Lane Nonnenberg, VP of Hewlett Packard; the author

These were very exciting days in the life of Unity Care. But as we expanded into multiple counties and implemented many new programs, the organization began to suffer from growing pains. When the staff challenged me to build a board of directors that could be more proactive about guiding us forward, I had to make some tough decisions. One was to exchange our founding board members and my childhood mentors, Mr. Roy Clay and Mr. Henry Ford, for younger talent who had the time, energy, and resources to support our aggressive growth strategy. We increased the size of the board from four members to twelve. I invited several of my former colleagues from the high-tech world to fill the empty slots.

Although I no longer had to travel across the country for my job, I was actually working harder than ever. Workweeks of sixty hours and more were typical, but the labor was more enjoyable and less taxing, because it was aligned with my passion.

Finding Your Purpose

In mid-2000, the Silicon Valley Community Foundation invited me to speak at a conference they hosted at Stanford University. The title of my talk was "Finding Your True Purpose and Passion in Giving."

"Take an inventory of your life and your strengths," I advised the two hundred executives in attendance. "Identify the things you do every day that give you energy. What types of activities do you do almost flawlessly? What are the things you're always eager to do, the things that cause the time to zoom by when you're doing them? Find the common denominator that runs through these activities. Then assess whether that passion can become a vocation that satisfies you from an economic, spiritual, and emotional perspective. Do your best to avoid the things that drain you."

After this talk, I was inundated with calls from senior executives who wanted to meet with me to find out how I had made the transition from the private sector to the non-profit sector. People who had been chasing the money began to reevaluate their life's purpose and search for deeper connections.

The calls became even more frequent when the dot-com bubble burst in 2001. As the over-inflated stock market crashed, a lot people in high-tech lost their jobs and their paper fortunes. Executives and venture capitalists that owned millions of dollars of stock in high-tech companies lost a large portion of that money almost overnight. To add insult to injury, many executives who had been granted stock at higher per-share prices had to pay taxes on money they never actually received.

The people who talked with me asked questions like, "What motivated you to go into non-profit work? How did you find your passion? Where did you get the courage to let go of the money? How did you resist the urge to change your mind and go back into high-tech?" A percentage of these people were really sincere about working in the non-profit sector, and a few even asked if I had a job for them at Unity Care. But I could tell that others were just looking for a place to land until the market rebounded.

Around 2002, a business executive approached me. "I want to do something good," he explained, "and I'm interviewing with different non-profit organizations. Can you give me some advice about how to approach this job transition?" I could tell as I shared my story that he was serious. Today he is executive director of the Boys and Girls Club of East Palo Alto. As far as I know, he is the only person I talked with who actually made the transition to non-profit work and resisted the temptation to return to the private sector.

A doctor came to me and said, "I love going to less-developed countries and helping the people. I wish I could do that full-time." I asked him some questions about the specifics of his situation, and he couldn't identify any significant obstacle that prevented him from pursuing his dream. Finally, I said to him, "The only thing that is stopping you is you. You've got to get out of the way of yourself."

I don't know what he decided to do, but it was clear that his deepest desires were in a life-and-death struggle with money and security. The challenge for all of us is to get out of the way of ourselves. Most of us can pursue our passion, if we simply take the initiative and do it.

Opening of Unity Care Computer Lab House #5, attended by our board of directors and local politicians. From the left, Chris Clay, Mayor Ron Gonzales, Councilman Forrest Williams, Ed Walker, Charlie Shea, Carl Agers, County Supervisor Jim Beall, Cedric Martin, and the author.

Once we start pursuing our passion, the momentum builds. As we see needs and help fulfill them, our eyes open to more needs, and our motivation to meet those needs increases. This is certainly what happened to me day after day, as I began to witness stories like Carl Wiseman's.

Carl's Story

Carl was a biracial child who entered the welfare system at age four. I met him when he was about ten. A local woman, who was so much a saint to many needy children in San Jose that people referred to her as "Mother Francis," often brought him to our church. A sweet and energetic child with a winning smile, Carl loved to run up and down the aisles, but underneath, he was traumatized and lonely. His father had died in prison, and his mother had died of AIDS. Like many foster children, he had bounced from home to home and school to school. His burning desire was to be part of a family where he would be wanted and loved.

At age fourteen, after progressing through the child welfare system to the juvenile justice system, Carl came to live at a Unity Care treatment home. During his stay with us, he stabilized his life and graduated from high school. At age eighteen, he decided to move to Reno, Nevada, to live with his cousins, in hopes of filling the emptiness of a family connection. Unfortunately, that move didn't work out, and after eight months he moved back to San Jose, homeless.

Between ages nineteen and twenty-four, he bounced between transitional housing programs, drop-in centers, and the county jail. When he was too old to receive transitional housing services, he slept anywhere he could: in his car, in the park, in the front lobby of our offices, and in homeless shelters. All the while, he kept looking for a job and, most of all, for some sense of self-worth.

Sadly, the harsh ailments arising from instability caught up with Carl, and he contracted pneumonia. I received a call from another former youth in our program, who informed me one day that Carl was in the hospital in a coma.

When I visited Carl, he was in ICU. The nurse said, "Who are you?" I said, "I'm his uncle." That was my usual response, because most of these kids refer to me as their uncle.

Carl had tubes everywhere, and he was non-responsive. I sat on the bed next to Carl, grabbed his hand and began to pray over him. I talked to him about how amazing he was, and I reminisced about some funny things that had happened when he was with us. At that moment, a tear came down his face, and I knew that he could hear me, and that whatever the outcome, God was in control.

After three weeks on life support, Carl died of congestive heart failure at age twenty-four. The community rallied to honor him. In less than a week, county social services staff, foundations, non-profit agencies, his former church, and various individuals contributed $4,000 for burial expenses. Nearly fifty people attended his funeral service, including many youths who shared Carl's circumstances. One young person told the gathering, "I came from the gutter, and that's all I know. But Carl inspired me, and I'm going try to get out."

Unfortunately, Carl's story is not unique. Each year in California, more than 4,500 foster care teenagers turn eighteen. What happens to these kids? Basically, the system abandons them to the streets, with the nonsensical expectation that they will somehow miraculously survive on their own with no support or stable family connections.

San Jose, where Unity Care is located, is in the heart of Silicon Valley, home to some of the brightest people in the world. Many are technology-made millionaires. One would think that this wealthy community of citizens could do better, but year after year it produces one of the fastest growing homeless populations in America.

The goal of the foster care system is to remove children from bad environments and place them in safe, stable, and nurturing ones, so they will grow up into productive adults. In reality, many of these youth move from the foster care system to the adult prison system.

In California, assembly members Jim Beall and Karen Bass[5], staunch advocates for foster care reform, introduced Assembly Bill 12, which tapped federal funding to extend foster care in the state of California from age eighteen to age twenty-one. We need more of this kind of political action. But if we're going to

[5] Today Jim Beall is a state senator, and Karen Bass is a congresswoman.

make real progress over the long term, we need to change our personal priorities as well. It's wonderful that a community raised $4,000 dollars in five days to bury Carl Wiseman, but Carl might be with us today if the community had given that same amount of compassion and money before he died. He could have paid his rent instead of living on the cold, treacherous streets.

CHAPTER 7

BREAKING UP IS HARD

If 60 percent of the products produced by Apple Computer, General Motors, or some other business failed within two to four years, customers and shareholders would rise up in arms. People would demand better. If the company didn't respond, it would soon be out of business. The government might even be called in to investigate.

With foster care, however, we seem to regard mediocre performance and failing outcomes as perfectly acceptable. It doesn't seem to bother us that within two to four years of youth aging out of foster care, 60 percent of these youth are either homeless, incarcerated, on drugs, pregnant, or suffering from significant mental health issues. The system is so detrimental to the children it's supposed to nurture and protect that it's become a pipeline to our prisons. Sadly, I've met some remarkable and committed social workers, managers, judges, and county leaders, who in spite of their good intentions, seem frustrated by the magnitude of the problems and are paralyzed into accepting the status quo.

When we herd foster children like cattle through ten, twenty, or even thirty different foster homes and almost as many different schools and neighborhoods before they turn eighteen, why are we surprised when many of them grow up to become victims of society's ills? When we focus on problem behaviors and fail to diagnose and treat the deeper issues that cause them, it's predictable that many foster kids will end up in our adult systems.

Children cannot pick their parents. It's not their fault if they were born into poverty and raised in broken homes and crime-ridden neighborhoods. These unfortunate children deserve a helping hand. With support, they can rise above their circumstances. Children are a gift from God, and they should be treated that way.

When children feel they are a liability, when they are not valued and not loved, is it any wonder most of them want to get as far away as possible from the adults when they turn eighteen? Their idea of adulthood is distorted by continuing uncertainty about whether they will ever have a safe place to live and a loving family that cares for them. When they're moved from one home to another, one school to another, and one neighborhood to another, the trauma can be overwhelming.

When foster children reach adulthood, for a brief time they may feel excited about being free to chart their own course. But the great majority of youths who "age out" of foster care are poorly prepared to live on their own, which is typical even for youths who grow up in supportive family environments. Their high expectations for a fulfilling life are shattered when they encounter the harsh realities of the world. In the face of overwhelming trauma, they are forced to rely on their instincts to survive. Not surprisingly, a great many make poor choices that lead to pregnancy, drug addiction, incarceration, and even prostitution and drug dealing.

Lost in the Labyrinth

One of our staff members, Joe Manly, is a football coach at the local high school. After practice one day, a fellow coach said to him, "I know that you work in foster care, and I wonder if you could help me locate my nephew. His name is Paul, and he's my mom's grandson. My mom is really ill, and I promised her that I would do my best to help her locate him. She's been looking for him for twelve years."

"I don't know if I can help," Joe answered, "but tell me the story."

"Paul's father died in an automobile accident," the other coach continued, "and his mother, my sister, suffered from schizophrenia. So, the State of California removed Paul from my sister's custody when he was two years old. We went to court and tried to get him placed with us, but they put him in foster care. Over the first couple of years, my mom stayed in contact with Paul as he was moved from the first foster home to a second, and then to a third, and then to a fourth. Around this time, he was assigned to a new social worker, and after a few more years, he was moved to another county. That's when we lost contact with him, and since then every attempt we've made to find him has been unsuccessful. The foster care system seems like a labyrinth with no way out. Can you help?"

"I'll see what I can do," said Joe. "What's the kid's last name?"

"Moraga. His name is Paul Moraga[6]," said the coach, adding a few more descriptive details.

"I know this kid!" exclaimed Joe. "He's in our program!"

It turned out that Paul Moraga, whom this family hadn't seen in fourteen years, had come to Unity Care when he was thirteen. He was now sixteen, and he was scheduled to stay in the foster care system until he was emancipated at age eighteen. Because his mother was out of the picture, any family information that existed was buried under years and years of court records and reports. There were no records in the system about the rest of Paul's natural family. Reunification with them was not part of the system's plan for him.

[6] This name has been changed to protect privacy.

When we connected Paul with his uncle and his grandmother, there was quite a celebration! But all stories don't end so well. Children like Paul are getting lost in the foster care system all the time. The point of contact in the court records is often just the mom, with most records reflecting "dad unknown" or "dad unresponsive."

If the situation between the social worker and the mom for some reason goes awry, the child can get swallowed up by the system and continue to move from foster home to foster home, and from social worker to social worker. The child's family history gets further buried with every new social worker, foster home, and court report, until it eventually disappears under hundreds of court reports. This situation caused us to consider what more we might have done to help Paul find his natural family.

In a few years, these children are well on the path to emancipation at age eighteen, with no connection in their records to their biological families. Understandably, family members can lose trust and get frustrated and angry at the system, because there's no way for them to learn where their children are. It feels to the children like the other family members have turned their backs on them, but in many cases grandparents, cousins, and other relatives would love to locate them and stay connected to them.

Of course, not all family members are able to take in additional children. For these situations, it is vital to have loving and caring foster and adoptive parents as options. But the primary emphasis should be on finding and restoring families.

Several of the youths in our program painted this and gave it to me with the words, "Even roses can grow out of concrete if watered and given the chance."

Finding Families

When I talk with people about foster care, I ask them, "How would you feel if your grandchild or nephew was taken away, and there was no way to find him? Would you lie awake at night wondering if he was scared, confused, hurt, and lonely? Would you worry that he might be in an environment that is uncomfortable, or possibly even dangerous or abusive?" I ask these questions to start people thinking about the downside of breaking up families.

The foster care system needs to place more emphasis on reconnecting foster children with natural family members. Yes, when there is substantial abuse and neglect, it is absolutely necessary and appropriate to remove children from their homes. When this is required, we should first focus on locating and providing support to uncles, aunts, grandparents, cousins, or other capable relatives who would be willing to open their homes. If an appropriate family member cannot be found, the child should be placed in a foster home or adoptive home.

The definition of family doesn't need to be restricted to the biological mother and father. It's been said that just about everyone has at least one hundred relatives. This opens up a great opportunity to get extended families involved, so these children are connected culturally at a time when they are experiencing significant trauma due to separation from their mother or father. The priority should be to restore children and families instead of separating them.

In 2008, President George W. Bush signed into law the Fostering Connections to Success and Increasing Adoptions Act. Championed by Kevin Campbell, founder of the Family Finding Model, its goal was to connect children removed from a home by child welfare services with other family members, so these children may benefit from the lifelong connections that only a family provides.

The law served as a nationwide catalyst for states and counties to set up "family finding" departments. These departments pulled the files on kids, many of whom had been languishing in the foster care system for years. Using the Internet and other modern technology, they located relatives of these children and started conversations with them about whether they'd consider becoming foster parents to them.

This program was a step in the right direction. In fact, it created a whole movement. But during the years following the 2009 economic dip, federal funding for this legislation dried up, and most states and counties were unable to maintain family finding practices. That's a shame, because finding families and connecting them with foster children is just basic common sense. Instead of treating family finding as a separate department or program, I believe it should be an integral part of child welfare services.

For every child under their care, social workers should be required to present to a judge a minimum of ten family members they've reached out to as potential guardians. These relatives can be uncles, aunts, nephews, nieces, second cousins, a second cousin's daughter, coaches, neighbors, or whoever else the child designates as family or friends. Social workers will often say they do not have time to focus on family finding, and it's true that locating and supporting relatives can be labor-intensive. But instead of tackling this task alone, counties should develop partnerships to enlist the help of churches, cultural brokers, and other community partners to provide on-going support to keep families together.

To improve the foster care system, we need to shift our perspective and view families through a strength-based lens rather than through a deficit-based lens. Then, we need to back up this more positive vision with adequate commitment and funding to aggressively enlist as many relatives as possible to be active participants in the child's life. This is fundamental to good social work, and it's what many social workers entered the field to do.

CHAPTER 8

CLOSING THE DOOR

Approximately 85 percent of families who enter the foster care system come through the same front door. This door is broad, and it's wide open. It sucks kids in like a black hole, and it's a primary reason why there is a disproportionally large number of African American and Latino children in foster care. The sign over the door reads "general neglect."

General neglect is the negligent failure of a parent/guardian or caretaker to provide adequate food, clothing, shelter, or supervision where no physical injury to the child has occurred. Unfortunately, child welfare agencies have broad discretion under the law about what constitutes general neglect, and that can lead to subjective, inconsistent, and sometimes inappropriate actions. Because the system leaves so much room for subjectivity, things like the background of the social worker can exert undue influence on what happens to families.

For example, consider a situation in which a social worker who was raised in an affluent community visits the home of a single mom who has been referred to social services because her children have had inconsistent attendance at school. When this social worker sees that the mom is raising four children in a crowed one-bedroom apartment, that she has no reliable transportation, and there is evidence of lack of food in the refrigerator, she might say to herself, "No child should live like this." She could then write a report to remove one or more of the children from that home on grounds of "general neglect."

Another social worker, more familiar with the culture of the community she serves, who perhaps even has lived with similar experiences, might decide that the situation in the home involves issues of well-being/poverty, not safety, and make a personal judgment that removing children from the home would be unnecessarily traumatic to the family unit. Instead of labeling the situation "general neglect," she might refer the family for prevention services to address well-being challenges and strengthen the family unit.

Millions of children of color across America are inappropriately bouncing around in the foster care system, simply because the term "general neglect" is so nebulous. I believe we should limit the scope of this term so there is a clear distinction between well-being/poverty issues and safety issues. Clear criteria should be developed and consistently applied across the system to reduce subjectivity. Underserved communities, unemployment, single family households, and lack of access to basic resources should be recognized as contributing factors that raise the level of risk to the families rather than resulting in the criminalization of poverty.

Before substantiating general neglect in these situations, the department of social services should seek other alternatives, such as expansion of differential response through community resources and partnerships. Differential response is a system reform that enables child protective services (CPS) to differentiate its response to reports of child abuse and neglect based on several factors. If a family fails to use the information and resources provided, or if the child's health or safety is at risk, child welfare interventions should be considered. I'll illustrate the difference with two examples.

Imagine a single mom with four kids, who is not at home in the evenings because she's working three jobs. She can't afford a babysitter or daycare, so she relies on her teenage daughter to care for her younger siblings. One afternoon, her daughter briefly goes into the house and leaves one of her younger siblings playing outside alone. A neighbor notices that this little boy is unsupervised and calls the police. The child welfare system gets involved and cites the mother for "neglect." The judge determines that she must attend a year of mandatory parenting classes in the evenings and be available for regular in-home visitations from the child welfare department during the day.

To comply with this requirement, this mother must give up one or more of her jobs. She must also pay for a babysitter, which puts her deeper in debt, raises the probability that she could lose her home, and significantly increases the family's stress. From that time forward, she will live in constant fear of having all of her children removed from her home and placed in foster care.

Right next door lives another single mother who also has four kids, but this mother spends her nights partying, drinking, and doing drugs with her boyfriend in front of her children. In the daytime, she sleeps off her hangover and relies on her teenage daughter to care for her younger siblings, who are often left unsupervised. A neighbor calls the police, and child welfare ends up citing this mom for "neglect." She is mandated to attend remedial parenting classes in the evenings, be at home for regular welfare department visitations, and attend substance-abuse classes.

Both of these mothers have come into the child welfare system through the exact same door: general neglect. Both are subject to the same court mandates, with the minor exception that the second mother must also attend substance abuse classes. But there's a major difference between these two cases that the welfare system fails to recognize.

The first mother's intentions are good, but her economic conditions prevent her from being at home to care for her children. The issues relate to the child's well-being, not to the child's safety. This mom needs help, not court-mandated oversight and programming. Directing her to attend remedial parenting classes in the evenings only exacerbates the problem. Breaking up the family and putting her children in foster care would unnecessarily traumatize the entire family and additionally burden the welfare system.

The issues with the second mother are much more serious, because they relate to safety. This mom clearly has a significant substance-use problem and no intention of putting the needs of her children ahead of her own personal desires. Her drug use presents a danger to her children. The best action for the protection of the children and the welfare of all concerned would be to remove the children from the home while mom receives the help she needs.

In most cases, our current child welfare policies will treat these two vastly different offenses exactly the same. The term "general neglect" should not automatically lead to intensified child welfare actions. It should not be a cause for removing children from the home and putting them in foster care. Rather, it should generate preemptive in-home prevention "wraparound services," in which a team of individuals who are relevant to the well-being of the child or youths (e.g., family members, other natural supports, service providers, and agency representatives) collaboratively develop an individualized plan of care, implement this plan, and evaluate success over time.

In these complex situations involving youths with the most serious emotional and behavioral problems in their home and community, the emphasis should be on intensive, individualized care designed to keep the family together. Well-being and poverty issues should not be lumped with safety issues under the umbrella of "general neglect." They are not sufficient reason to open a child welfare case, begin legal actions, and remove children from their parents.

Acting Instead of Reacting

For the most part, government agencies are funded to put out fires, not prevent them. They wait until a situation has become desperate before taking action.

Suppose you're a parent of a child who is doing very poorly at school. What would the school system do? A good teacher would immediately inform you, so you could arrange for tutoring and initiate other supportive actions. In other words, you and the school would cooperatively take a proactive, failure-prevention approach.

The child welfare system typically operates very differently. Rather than taking proactive steps to prevent failure, it waits for failure to occur and then reacts. If the school in our example operated like the welfare system, it would wait until your child gets an F at the end of the term. Then it would call you in for a chat about having your child repeat the course, or even repeat the entire year.

To use another analogy, if you as a parent notice that your child continually has a cough and a runny nose, you'll probably try to identify the cause. If you discover, for example, that she hasn't been wearing her jacket while playing outside, you'd probably teach her how to properly dress. But government agencies tend to concentrate on treating symptoms rather than causes. For example, if the child welfare system were this parent, it would simply give the child lots of medicine to try to control the cold's symptoms. Only when the child ends up in the hospital would it initiate more impactful interventions.

With the "fail-up, deficit-based" philosophy of our current child welfare system, the more a family fails, the higher up the social services ladder it goes. The bigger the deficits, the greater the array of services the family can access.

This approach results in some really nonsensical actions. For instance, child welfare agencies may cite parents for being neglectful or abusive, just so they can qualify for social services and receive necessary funding. If a mom has been unable to pay the rent because she's been unable to get a job, and she's been unable to get a job because she has to take care of four children, the state may think it's providing this mom and society a service by citing this mom with "neglect" and taking one or more children off her hands.

In her excellent article titled "Prison, Foster Care, and the Systemic Punishment of Black Mothers,"[7] Dorothy E. Roberts, the George A. Weiss University Professor of Law & Sociology at the University of Pennsylvania, argues that excess punishment of black mothers by the U.S. prison system and the foster care system actually promotes and preserves race, gender, and class inequality. According to Roberts, over-policing in recent decades has resulted in the simultaneous explosion of both the prison and foster care populations, to the severe detriment of black communities. She analyzes how state mechanisms of surveillance and punishment function jointly to penalize the most marginalized women in our society, while blaming them for their own disadvantaged positions.

Ms. Roberts points out that prior to the Civil Rights Movement, African American children were disproportionately excluded from child welfare services, which catered mainly to white families. By 2000, however, African American children were the largest group in foster care. Even though they comprise only about 15 percent of the nation's children, black children currently compose about 30 percent of the nation's foster care population.

For the past thirty years, the harsh criminal penalties of the war on drugs have disproportionately penalized the African American community. Today, our nation is experiencing an even worse drug crisis: the opioid epidemic. It is forcing tens of thousands of children across the country into the foster care system.

[7] Dorothy E. Roberts, "Prison, Foster Care, and the Systemic Punishment of Black Mothers," 59 *UCLA Law Review* 1474 (2012)

According to National Public Radio, "The crisis is so severe — with a 32 percent spike in drug-related cases from 2012 to 2016 — that it reversed a decade-long trend in which the foster care system had been shrinking in size. All told, about 274,000 children entered foster care in the U.S. last year. A total of 437,000 children were in the system as of Sept. 30, 2016."[8]

More than 80 percent of opioid overdose victims are white, and it's interesting to see how differently the government is responding to this crisis compared to the way it responded to the crack cocaine crisis. The crack epidemic that devastated the African American community was predominantly considered a criminal issue, while this recent opioid epidemic is addressed primarily as a health issue. With opioid overdose victims, the focus is on treatment instead of on incarceration.

A New Way of Thinking

Over the past two decades, I've worked alongside some of the brightest child welfare staff in the industry, and I've heard them express many of the frustrations I have voiced in these pages. They've asked many of the same questions I've raised about how we can think differently about families, so we keep them together instead of breaking them apart.

Overwhelming caseloads prevent even the best social workers from addressing many of these issues. The courts are responsible for the ultimate decisions, and they are burdened with overwhelming caseloads and crowded dockets, which make it difficult for judges and attorneys to make informed decisions. All of these factors taken together demonstrate why the system is broken and why a new way of thinking is needed.

A variety of preventive initiatives have had some success. Differential response is one example. It has the potential to provide some of the radical wholesale systemic change that's needed to reorient the system in the right direction.

Our goal should be to provide preventative in-home support services to parents and/or other primary caregivers before more drastic measures are necessary. This philosophical change in how we operate child welfare would also dramatically reduce the number of children who are removed from families and forced to grow up in a dysfunctional foster care system.

The current reactive, deficit-based, fail-up approach of our children serving systems doesn't make sense. Considerable research demonstrates that it's better and more economical over the long run to proactively identify the root causes of social problems and provide the resources to correct them. This is true in all areas of government human service agencies. For instance, going upstream and finding housing for homeless people saves considerable money downstream in medical

[8] https://www.npr.org/2017/12/23/573021632/the-foster-care-system-is-flooded-with-children-of-the-opioid-epidemic

costs, police calls, prisons stays, and so on. Likewise, teaching kids reading and study skills prior to the third grade produces a large return on investment for society in future years. We should be providing these kinds of preventive services for the less fortunate families in our society who struggle with poverty and well-being issues.

We don't help these families when we bring their children into the child welfare system for general neglect issues related only to well-being and poverty. That only adds the additional burdens of social worker compliance, court appearances, and other mandates to their already stressful lives. We should support these families with counseling, financial assistance, employment, housing, education, and in other ways, so they can get on their feet. The right approach is to shift the funding and create polices that move upstream and deal with the root causes. This will reduce the risk factors that are driving families down, so their children don't eventually end up in a broken child welfare system.

Useful data about the health, social, and economic risks that result from childhood trauma is emerging from an on-going collaborative research project between the Centers for Disease Control and Prevention, headquartered in Atlanta, GA, and Kaiser Permanente of San Diego, CA. This Adverse Childhood Experiences (ACE) study involving over 17,000 Kaiser patients shows that minimizing adverse childhood experiences, or "ACEs," is key to maximizing chances of success in life.[9] To minimize ACEs, the child welfare system must radically change the way it approaches its work. It must begin to focus on root causes instead of symptoms.

What's the Problem?

So, why don't state and local governments seek to proactively minimize trauma in children's lives? Why do we wait until trauma has occurred before providing services?

The typical response from government officials is, "Yes, we agree that issues need to be addressed before they become problems, but funding restrictions prevent us from going upstream. We have limited funds for preventive services, and we can't shortchange that." But this philosophy is like a teacher who tells a parent that her son can't get after-school tutoring until he flunks. It's an ineffective strategy that perpetuates a broken system which keeps failing our children.

One remedy for this failed system is to loosen the restrictions around how federal money flows to the states. States and counties need the freedom to use funds for prevention, instead of simply for intervention. Fortunately, the federal government has responded to this need for greater flexibility by creating the "Title IV-E Waiver" program. Any state can apply to participate in this program, and once the state's application has been approved, any county within the state can opt in.

[9] https://www.cdc.gov/violenceprevention/acestudy/about.html

Here's how it works: instead of receiving a certain amount of child welfare money per child from the federal government, the county agrees to accept a block grant based on the prior three years' expenditures for child welfare. Once the county receives this grant, it has the freedom to use the funds for any child welfare programs it desires, including preventive care. The catch, if you can call it that, is that the county will receive no more money from the federal government for that year, even if its child welfare population increases. Essentially, the county is betting that greater flexibility in the use of funds will enable it to hold the line on child welfare costs, or possibly even reduce them.

When counties have more control over how they spend their child welfare funds, they generally allocate more of them for preventive services, such as federal differential response programs, flex funding, housing subsidies, mental health services, and health education. In other words, they focus primarily on causes rather than symptoms. Let's push our federal government to give our states the flexibility they need to be innovative and go upstream to expand preventive services.

A Declaration of Hope

Frank L. Alexander, director of the Boulder County Department of Housing and Human Services, is among a growing number of leaders who have come to recognize the importance of infusing communities with hope. More and more leaders are asking the question, "What if we could invest more of our federal child welfare funding in preventing child abuse and neglect, rather than placing children in foster care?"

Dr. William C. Bell, president and CEO of Casey Family Programs, a Seattle-based non-profit that provides strategic consulting to child welfare systems and community partners throughout the United States and beyond, is contributing enormously to the dialog. "The power to build hope rests in the collective will of a community and its families," says Dr. Bell. "We need to understand the interdependencies among families, neighborhoods, schools, local businesses, law enforcement, churches and non-profits."

Dr. Bell argues that we also need to acknowledge the importance of coordination among governmental sectors such as the judiciary, education, health, and human services, as well as the role that philanthropy and business plays in supporting strategies that improve the lives of children and families.

"When you see the safety of children as directly related to the strength of their families and the support of their communities, the dialogue around child welfare begins to change," observes Dr. Bell. "New questions about our collective responsibility begin to arise. How can we keep more children safe from abuse and neglect? How can we ensure children grow up in safe, permanent, and stable families rather than in foster care? How can we strengthen families and extended families, so they are better able to raise their own children successfully? How can communities provide the resources and support that families need to raise their children in safe environments – both in and outside their homes? And how can we ensure that no child ever ages out of the foster care system?"

Dr. Bell goes on to say that the answers to these questions are evolving. "They are being informed by the power of data to reveal new insights into the specific needs of children in foster care. They are being enhanced by advances in brain science and new approaches, such as trauma-informed care, that are helping to heal the often hidden and painful wounds of adverse childhood experiences. And they are being shaped by a richer understanding of how policies and practices need to keep pace with advances in our understanding of child development, so we can invest resources more effectively at a national, state, and local level to better prevent abuse and neglect in the first place."

"Too often, we respond to child victims of violence within the narrow confines of child-centered intervention strategies," says Dr. Bell. "We fail to recognize and deal with the factors that affect the families and communities where those children live. We cannot resolve child maltreatment and its related issues in silos. To make any lasting headway in preventing child abuse and neglect, and in treating its devastating effects, we must consistently view children in the context of their families, view families in the context of their communities, and view any intervention—and its funding—in the context of a family and community-support network.

"It is through this holistic approach that we will build a solid platform that can ensure the safety and success of every child in America. It is within this approach that we will create a lasting Declaration of Hope for all of our children."

I have quoted Dr. Bell at length because his insights are so accurate. Just think how much better off our society would be if we could demolish our current foster care system and rebuild it along the lines he has articulated! If we focused more on engaging communities and supporting them in strengthening families, we would see amazing advances in the safety and well-being of our children. We do not need to traumatize youths and families. We have the knowledge to protect and nurture them. We just need the will to act on that knowledge.

CHAPTER 9

FIXING THE SYSTEM

When I left the private sector to begin working full-time at Unity Care, my performance expectations created some friction. Admittedly, I was too demanding. I needed to learn that managing an organization that serves people is very different from managing a high-tech software sales team. Nevertheless, I knew that to be successful, Unity Care had to change its culture. When some of my staff pushed back with, "We're non-profit. We don't operate that way," I reminded them that non-profit is merely a tax code, not a business model. Unity Care should operate with the same level of excellence and accountability as a for-profit company.

The type of non-urgent or non-pressing attitude I was confronting at Unity Care infects a great many non-profit and government entities, especially in the human services sector. I've been to hundreds of meetings of these organizations, and typically the inefficiencies stick out like sore thumbs. Even the culture of dialog in human services agencies is very different from the culture of dialog in the private sector. In human services, it tends to be more relational and congenial, while in for-profit organizations, it's generally more transparent and courageous.

The managers in these government agencies are some of the industry's best and brightest. They have valuable skills and good intentions, but they often lack the facts-focused, results-oriented attitude required for success in the business world. In private industry, most managers have a business school education or some other form of formal management training. As they move up the ladder, companies invest considerable time and money equipping them for increasingly higher levels of effective leadership.

It's been my observation that a large percentage of managers in government, especially in state, county, and city services, never aspired to be in charge of major departments. Many were excellent individual contributors or social workers who kept getting promoted up the ranks, until one day they found themselves handling responsibilities that exceeded their leadership expertise. They were simply expected to perform well with no formal management training, except for perhaps a few one-day or one-week workshops.

The primary fault lies not with these managers, but with the system. If government and non-profit agencies followed the example of the private sector and did a better job of preparing and training talented performers for leadership responsibilities, the effectiveness of the services they provide to children and families would increase dramatically. This is an area of great need and great opportunity.

Private sector companies and non-profit organizations have many more similarities than differences. Both must produce and market services, manage people, maintain budgets, and meet a host of regulatory requirements. The former seeks to satisfy customers and stockholders, with the goal of maximizing return on investment (ROI). The latter seeks to satisfy government funders, clients, donors, and communities, with the goal of maximizing their "social return on investment" (SROI). There's no reason why non-profit organizations can't train their leaders to operate more like their counterparts in the private sector in terms of effectiveness and efficiency. The "hard-science skills" of the business world are not incompatible with the "soft skills" of the helping professions. Over the past decade, we've witnessed the rise of social entrepreneurs and the conversion of technology and non-profits focused on social impact. Child welfare agencies can learn from these examples.

Outputs vs. Outcomes

Successful private companies aim to correct problems at the source. For example, if an airline notices that customer complaints are rising, it won't merely focus on trying to make the unhappy customers feel better. Rather, it will dive in and examine the entire supply chain, until it locates and corrects the source of the problem.

Government human services agencies typically concentrate more on the effects of problems than on the causes. For example, most cities will address the problem of homelessness by seeking to "help" the homeless people, instead of seeking to correct the problems that caused the people to become homeless. Addressing symptoms instead of causes does little more than assuage guilt. That's why homeless rates in most cities persist at the same or higher levels year after year.

I've talked to a lot of managers of government agencies about looking further upstream to address the root causes of problems, but they're content to live with the status quo. One particular child welfare director I greatly respect once told me, "André, we can't control who comes to our front door. The problems exist in our society before they hit our doors."

Many leaders in the non-profit sector agree that the need is urgent, and some even struggle to do things differently. But the system itself is entrenched in the status quo. It refuses to delve deeply into underserved communities where, according to the data, the highest number of entries into the child welfare system originate. The notion of alleviating pains rather than eliminating the causes of those pains is just too ingrained in the culture. Year after year, government agencies continue to tolerate huge inefficiencies and assume they can't do any better.

Social return on investment (SROI) and accountability for outcomes are unfamiliar concepts to many state, county, and city government agencies. Instead of identifying measurements that support their mission, they madly run around trying to measure just about everything else. But as Albert Einstein said, "Everything that can be counted does not necessarily count; everything that counts cannot necessarily be counted."

The federal government has told the state of California, which then has told the counties in the state, to measure the number of contacts social workers have with each family. The implicit assumption is that three visits per month to a family are better than one. However, this is not necessarily true. One visit focused on measurable outcomes may do more good than three check-in visits with a lack of engagement.

Recording quantity of visits with no consideration of quality merely adds to the paperwork overload. It does not ensure higher quality outcomes, nor does it necessarily improve service. No wonder many non-profit organizations view performance based management as an unnecessary burden rather than a helpful tool! It simply adds to the paperwork when performance is measured by activities instead of results.

Many government institutions and non-profit agencies seem to have difficulty understanding and appreciating the difference between an output, which is a measurement of an activity level, and an outcome, which is a measurement of a life impact. For example, the number of kids who show up for a financial literacy class would be an output measurement. The number of kids in that class motivated to open a bank account and develop a personal budget with the goal of saving money is an outcome measurement. Measuring outputs is not an effective means of motivating workers and gauging progress. If the output is not connected to an outcome, measuring it merely adds to the organization's administrative burden.

In private industry, companies or departments that don't produce results get dealt with pretty quickly. Investors won't keep funding a unit that doesn't produce a profit. Government institutions, however, don't have that degree of accountability. They're funded by taxpayer collections, whether or not they produce results.

In many cases, government and non-profit organizations don't have the funding to build the organizational capacity, acquire the technological infrastructure, and hire the intellectual talent to develop robust outcome systems. As I mentioned earlier, this is where we see the collision between the "hard-science skills" of the business world, where data is ingrained in the culture, with the "soft skills" of the helping professions, which struggle to understand outputs and outcomes.

Encouraging Trends

Fortunately, things are changing. More and more government agencies, especially at the federal and state levels, are making funding contingent on measurable outcomes. The Title IV-E Waiver program in foster care, which I discussed in the last chapter, has been a catalyst for a number of innovative approaches around the country that shift child welfare resources toward prevention and early intervention.

Over the past several years, the good news is that federal and state governments have promoted greater accountability. Social Impact Bonds (SIBs), for example, are an innovative financing vehicle for social programs that incorporate performance-based funding. With SIBs, the external social service organization providing the service to the government absorbs the risk associated with achieving an agreed-upon outcome. In this sense, it acts somewhat like a venture capitalist would in the private sector.[10]

The social service organization, which can be either a for-profit or non-profit organization, enters into a contract (bond) with the government agency to achieve specific outcomes for a specified amount of funding. These outcomes are often measured in terms of savings, but other benchmarks can be used. If the social service organization achieves the outcomes, it gets the agreed-upon funding. If it doesn't, it gets nothing.

Because the government agency places few, if any, controls on how the outcome is to be achieved, the social service organization has the freedom to address the fundamental causes of the problems, not just their effects. SIBs typically cover periods of three to five years, so the organization has sufficient time to look further upstream and take actions that will result in long-term favorable outcomes. Because the external organization is assuming the risk, it will usually be entitled to a bigger reward if it exceeds expectations, much like a venture capital firm will benefit if its investment in a private company generates a large return on investment. The money for the government agency's payoff to the social service organization will usually come from the savings that the social service organization achieves for the government agency.

SIBs have very effectively brought together government agencies, social service providers, and philanthropists to help mitigate such problems as homelessness in cities, recidivism in prison systems, and the detrimental health impacts

---

[10] For more information on this subject, see the excellent article "What Are Social Impact Bonds?" by Jitinder Kohli, Douglas J. Besharov, and Kristina Costa, published by the Center for American Progress, March 22, 2012   https://www.law.upenn.edu/cf/faculty/roberts1/workingpapers/59 UCLALRev1474(2012).pdf

of smoking and obesity. The foster care system is especially fertile ground for innovative financing that incentivizes imaginative solutions to problems further upstream, closer to their source.

Social service organizations have an opportunity to survive and flourish in today's new environment of accountability by operating more like private sector businesses. They would do well to view efficiency and effectiveness as goals and mediocrity as unacceptable. Focusing more on outcomes would allow them to better meet the needs of the clients and communities they are committed to serve.

A Paradigm of Service

When people shop at a high quality retail clothing store, eat at a fine restaurant, or stay in a nice hotel, they expect to be treated with courtesy and respect. Why shouldn't we expect the same type of treatment from the formal systems that provide services to our children and families? Although a majority of social workers are compassionate and well-meaning, the culture of the system focuses on clients' deficits. This creates a culture of blame, shame, and fault-finding, which unintentionally marginalizes the children and families it's supposed to be supporting.

Social service organizations typically offer highly personal services that can dramatically impact the lives of people in need, and they will usually maintain a relationship with these clients over a long period. Retail establishments, in contrast, typically conduct short-term, rather impersonal commercial transactions with customers they may never see again. Which one of these two providers of services do you think would provide better customer service? Unfortunately, even average retail establishments usually provide better customer service than most child welfare agencies.

Government agencies need a paradigm shift in the way they view their mission. They need to become agencies of healing that display a welcoming attitude and have a deep understanding of the impact of trauma. Their priority should be to empower the people they serve, not to exercise power over them. Their goal should be to value, honor, and respect their clients, not marginalize them. Holding their clients accountable is important, but serving their clients well, especially by helping them deal with trauma, is even more important.

Ideally, the structure of the service organization should be designed to reinforce this servant attitude. For example, let's assume I'm a social worker who earns $100 a day for serving ten different clients. If my boss pays me $100 at the end of each day, I may provide good service to these clients. If I get paid by collecting $10 from each client, I will provide great customer service, because if I don't, the clients won't pay me. The system itself encourages me to provide good service and show respect.

Of course, it's difficult to institutionalize this kind of reinforcement within government child welfare agencies, because a disconnect exists between the work provided and the payments received. A social worker will receive the same amount of pay, regardless of the quality of the service provided. If the service is poor, the people receiving it are in a rather weak position to complain.

Even though most social workers come into this field with a desire to help people better themselves, they work within a deficit-based culture that doesn't reward or incentivize good customer service. Over the years, I've heard some phenomenally compassionate social workers who felt stuck by the culture of the system say, "We have to leave our culture in our car when we come to work."

We will get better overall results by building incentives into the structure of the welfare delivery system. I suggest we do this by borrowing some ideas from the private sector. The private sector understands and appreciates the value of superior customer service. Most for-profit companies strive to demonstrate their care for customers by courteously and effectively serving them. Shouldn't governmental organizations cultivate the same type of customer-focused culture?

If we look at some of the private companies that have the highest rating for their customer service and customer experience, such as Amazon, Hilton, Marriott, Chick-Fil-A, Trader Joe's, UPS, and Virgin Airlines, we find a few common themes. Each one of these companies has created an authentic culture of engagement that gives highest priority to the needs of its customers. The philosophy of "people first and profits second" is infused into every aspect of their business practices. They know that without customers, they will make no sales; without sales, they will have no cash flow; and without cash flow, they will go out of business.

Housing Industry Foundation (HIF) volunteers who renovated one of our transitional homes as a community service project.

Although the government often has a monopoly in the services it provides, and its funds come indirectly through taxes rather than directly in payments from clients, I believe it should be possible for these institutions to incorporate some features of the competitive marketplace into the public sector. If government agencies were required to obtain feedback from their customers on the services they rendered, for example, and if their managers were to some degree rewarded based on this feedback, we'd see a noticeable improvement in service quality.

Government entities and non-profit agencies tend to prioritize regulatory compliance over operational effectiveness. They focus excessive attention on reducing the administrative overhead of the non-profits to which they allocate funds, even though this very overhead is critical to building sustainable systems that produce measurable outcomes.

For example, if an agency that receives a $50,000 contract spends $45,000 on direct services and $5,000 on administrative overhead, the governmental entity that awarded the contract will be more interested in how the agency spent the $5,000 than in how well it spent the $45,000 as measured in positive impact. The government should learn from the private business sector about the importance of investing in operations to scale capacity and improve service.

Performance-based contracting is a healthy step toward introducing account-ability for outcomes into the non-profit sector. Unfortunately, most agencies adopt this approach only when it's required by federal, state, county, and city govern-ments. It will be a real sign of progress when more government agencies start investing in operations, instituting accountability of outcomes, not simply to meet funding requirements, but because, through their own initiative, they want to im-prove operations, services, and client outcomes.

We can accelerate the shift to a paradigm of service by making the foster care system more transparent. If recipients of services had access to their court and client records, so they could see what their social workers and caregivers were saying about them, I believe putting the family in the center would revolutionize the quality of care.

Imagine how differently a worker would write a report if he knew the fam-ily he was serving was going to read it. For example, instead of simply recording that the mom missed five family visits, which focuses on her deficits, the worker will be motivated to understand why the mom missed five family visits, while acknowledging all her strengths. Then, he will want to record any mitigating cir-cumstances, along with his positive recommendations for improvement. We've seen how this type of shift toward greater ownership and partnership can benefit both client and practitioner in the medical field, where the introduction of patient portals has put patients at the center of their care.

I am convinced this kind of transparency would totally transform the dynam-ics of the social worker, caregiver and client relationship. It would shift the social worker and caregiver's focus from recording deficiencies so more supportive services can be provided (the mechanism of our current "fail up" system) to recording strengths and talents so challenges can be addressed and ameliorated.

Instead of writing a report about the client, the systems provider will write the report with the client. Instead of interacting with the client from a position of domination and control, the worker will serve the client from a perspective of cooperation and healing.

As mentioned above, the medical field already provides patients with this type of access to records through their electronic health records and web-based portals. Patients can access their medical history online at any time and see everything in their patient files, as well as what their doctors are saying about them. I believe we must provide better customer service in foster care, and I believe we can by introducing the type of transparency that exists in the medical field.

CHAPTER 10

ENGAGING COMMUNITIES OF COLOR

Our views and behaviors are shaped largely by the culture in which we are raised. When people from different cultures interact, misunderstandings can occur that lead to tensions and mistrust. For example, I'm quite certain that if I were to go onto a reservation to work with Native Americans, it wouldn't take me long to unintentionally cause some hurt or even disrespect due to my lack of knowledge about their culture and customs.

Unfortunately, these types of cultural misunderstandings are often in evidence across America. This is especially true when the makeup of government institutions does not reflect the communities they serve. We see them played out, for example, in the racial conflicts between some communities and their police departments. These types of cultural misunderstandings happen far too often in the context of government social service programs. There has never been a time in this country's history where the African American male has not been under attack by our formal systems. Going back to slavery, Jim Crow, the Civil Rights Era and the rise of white supremacy in America, our communities of color have been under attack.

Human service agencies and non-profit providers can increase their engagement and better build trust with families and communities they serve when they truly understand the historical, multi-dimensional dynamics that have shaped their values and traditions. Particularly when working in African American communities, they need to be well-informed about the social and economic biases deeply entrenched in America's institutions. There needs to be greater recognition and appreciation for how opportunities and resources have been inequitably divided along racial lines for generations.

When systems ignore these cultural facts, they can unintentionally retraumatize African American families, causing resistance and possibly even antagonism. I've read thousands of court reports that list the father as "unknown" and only focus on supporting the mother. This is often a result of the systemic biases against the males. We must aggressively work to change the system, so it devotes the same level of intent, resources, and support to engaging the fathers as it devotes to engaging the mothers.

In his excellent book, *Community,* Peter Block makes the case that formal systems are capable of service, but not care. "As soon as you professionalize care, you have produced an oxymoron," Block argues. "Talk to any poor person or vulnerable person, and they will give you a long list of the services they have received. They are well serviced, but you often have to ask what in their life has fundamentally changed."[11]

I wholeheartedly agree. To a significant extent, I believe one reason why formal systems cannot provide care is because they ignore the lessons of history. They overlook the extent to which communities, especially communities of color, have drawn their fortitude largely from their spiritual roots. Spirituality is what held African Americans together as they endured slavery, the Jim Crow era, and the struggles of the Civil Rights Movement. Spirituality has been the primary source of their strength, hope, perseverance, resiliency, and cohesiveness. Spirituality enabled them to persevere through enormous trials and tribulations.

People are often reluctant to talk about spiritual issues, but they undergird every culture. If the child welfare system wants to increase its engagement with minority communities and help rebuild their families, it should strengthen and formalize opportunities with faith-based agencies to incorporate the spiritual dimension into their work. How can a government system that doesn't recognize the role of the church successfully help communities who, for generations, have relied on their spiritual roots to overcome hardships?

Although much excellent work has been conducted by faith-based entities for youths, the government-based social service system is deficit-based. It focuses on what's missing. Faith communities, on the other hand, are worth-based. They remind us that we all have worth, because God created us all in His image. Authentic faith focuses on forgiveness, not judgment, and on people's potential, not their deficiencies. Faith-based communities are an ideal complement for the social service system. They offer help, not hurt.

At Unity Care, spirituality is a vital component of our programs and services. Our management philosophy is based on servant leadership. As servant leaders, we believe our first priority is to serve those who enter our doors with compassion and understanding. Every day we rely on God's faithfulness and power to do this important work. When we tell kids they are a blessing from the Lord, that they are not a mistake, and that God created them with a vision and a purpose, we genuinely mean it.

None of us can pick our parents, so we constantly remind youths in our care that they are special, not only to us, but more importantly to God. We remind them that when they are going through a hard time, and when no one else

[11] Peter Block, *Community: The Structure of Belonging* (San Francisco: Berrett-Koehelr Publishing, 2009)

is there for them, God is always there. They can always go to Him in prayer, and He will give them guidance, strength, and peace in the midst of their trial. Families and youths need to hear this. If you've experienced little or no love in your life, imagine how it feels to learn that God loves you and that your life has worth and purpose.

Over the years, social workers have repeatedly told me that Unity Care's workers need to "leave their spirituality in the car" when they go into families' homes. They're not supposed to bring up religion or spirituality, which means, for example, that they should not pray with families in need. How can social service workers truly create trusting relationships with families without the ability to break bread with them? This is one reason why a formal system is unable to provide care.

Unity Care staff at our annual Town Hall Celebration event

An Appropriate Balance

Especially in the early days of Unity Care, a few social workers would give us a hard time about the way we integrated faith into our programs and services. One particular social worker used to call me and say, "André, you can't force the kids to go to church every Sunday. You're violating their personal rights and the separation of church and state. If you don't stop, I'm going to report you."

"We aren't forcing kids to go to any particular church, or even to go to church at all," I'd explain. "Any kid is free to stay home, and other kids are free to go to the church of their choice. The only difference is that youths who stay home will also miss the Sunday dinner out and the trip to the mall, the baseball game, or whatever other activities we do after church."

Every six months or so for several years, this one particular social worker pushed back against our practice of taking youths to church. At one point, he even complained to the county social services director. Nothing ever came of it, and we continued integrating faith into our programs in appropriate ways that respected the kids' freedom to choose their religious views and practices.

After a while, the pushback stopped. For about six or seven years, we didn't hear anything from the county about separation of church and state. Then, one day I received a notice that the Department of Mental Health was offering a training session on how to incorporate spirituality into a family's treatment goals. This surprised me, because it was the first time to my knowledge that a government agency had acknowledged the importance of the spiritual dimension of families. I immediately signed up to attend.

When I showed up for the training, I was shocked to see the social worker who used to give me so much grief about our supposed violations of the separation of church and state. After the workshop, I went up to speak with him.

"André," he said as I approached, "I know what you're going to say, and I know this information isn't new to you. You and your staff have been doing this for a long time. But this is now something you have to include in your treatment plan."

"I'm glad you've come over to the right side," I replied. He never said what caused him to change his mind, and I didn't ask. I was just glad to see that the county was finally recognizing that spirituality is a vital component of a family's life.

I believe government systems have a greater opportunity to succeed when they have a foundational spiritual component to their service model. They can acquire this spiritual component by proactively and enthusiastically embracing faith-based agencies and churches. Much like our hospitals have chaplains and places for prayer for families in need, so should our government service agencies provide spiritual support to hurting families.

Prioritizing Self-Sufficiency

Our goal at Unity Care is to work ourselves out of a job. We want the children and families who graduate from our programs to be self-sufficient. We want them to be able to live successful lives on their own, without being dependent on us or on any formal government system. That's one reason why we build strong relationships with neighborhood places of worship, while encouraging our families to connect with their natural support systems.

Even in today's environment of hypersensitivity to the separation of church and state, there are many opportunities for religious organizations to effectively work with government agencies and other secular social service institutions. They can offer vital love and compassion as foster parents, adoptive parents, counselors, and mentors to hurting families.

At Unity Care, we intentionally reach out to faith communities, and many churches come to us asking how they can help. Some end up adopting our programs and treatment homes and help make improvements to their facilities. Others serve as mentors to our kids, cook Thanksgiving or Christmas dinners for them, offer them jobs, provide them with educational support, or even teach them how to quilt. These are just a few of the ways faith-based communities interact with us.

Ribbon cutting ceremony at opening of Los Gatos Home for Girls. From left: State Senator Jim Beall; Beth Wyman, Mary-Lyle Rempel & Nancy Castro with West Valley Open Door Foundation; the author; Veronica, Bill Del Biaggio, chairman of the board of Heritage Bank; Ash Kalra, San Jose city councilmember

Every volunteer who wants to work with our kids on a regular basis must go through a background check and special training to learn what is permissible and what isn't. In these training sessions, we help them understand the trauma of growing up in foster care. We stress the importance of maintaining professional boundaries, being a blessing, and having a servant's attitude with a nonjudgmental attitude toward youths and families.

Safeguarding Against Trauma

Foster care is supposed to protect children from cruel neglect and abuse inflicted by adults. Study after study has shown that children suffer severe trauma when they are removed from the home and placed in foster care. Forced dislocation can instigate an array of psychological problems and personality disorders, including lifelong issues of mistrust and fear of abandonment.[12][13]

The child welfare department in our county operates out of a beautiful, modern, five-story glass structure. It's a wonderful place to work, and aesthetically it even rivals some of the local high-tech campuses. Unfortunately, as is common with too many government buildings, it fails to provide families with a culturally proficient welcoming environment. In fact, its design unintentionally adds to their trauma.

The problem starts in the waiting area of the front lobby. As parents sit in chairs aligned in rows waiting for their social worker to appear from behind glass doors, their children have no place to play except on the hard floor. The waiting area is fully visible to everyone who enters the building. Imagine how

[12] http://usatoday30.usatoday.com/news/nation/2007-07-02-foster-study_N.htm#Close
[13] http://www.nccpr.org/reports/evidence.pdf

embarrassed you would feel if you were sitting in this waiting area because of an open child abuse case, and your neighbor, a work colleague, a parent of your child's classmate, or someone else you knew walked by.

One day as I was entering this building to attend a meeting, I saw a member of my church in this waiting area. She tried to turn away to avoid making eye contact with me, and I obliged her. She obviously didn't want me to know that she might have been cited for child abuse. Even though I deal with child abuse cases every day, I was embarrassed for her.

Because social workers have so much power over the people they serve, they can easily create trauma in the lives of families without realizing it. Simply receiving a summons to come to a social services office is a traumatic event for most families. The family's anxiety will increase during the drive to the office building. It will ratchet up another notch as the family sits in the waiting room, and it will spike even more as they sit down across the desk from the social worker. Imagine how much more the family would open up and enter into honest, constructive dialog if the meeting could take place in the family's home, the family's church, or even at a community center on a Saturday or Sunday.

If visiting a social worker's office is stressful, just imagine how traumatic it is for children and families when police sweep into the family's home like a SWAT team and lead a parent off in handcuffs. Social workers at some point will talk with the children and the family about the trauma they experienced living with their "abusive or neglectful" parent, but we often fail to consider the trauma the children experienced when the police invaded the family's home and took their daddy away in handcuffs! That image will be forever in the minds of those children who experienced the trauma of that situation.

Children who live in communities characterized by poverty, unemployment, homelessness, shootings, drug dealings, and other traumatic experiences often acquire amazing resiliency and an exceptional ability to overcome adversity. But these victims of trauma may also become detached from reality as a means of survival. Consequently, they may have little ability to recognize and discuss the negative effects that these traumatic experiences have had on their lives. In making service referrals and plans, social workers and care providers should know how to use trauma screening and other assessments to help children and families identify sources of trauma and understand their impact.

Our children-serving systems and the providers that labor in them need to be more trauma-informed. There needs to be more awareness about what causes trauma, how to avoid inflicting even more trauma, and how to help facilitate recovery from trauma when it occurs. Training in historical trauma awareness and treatment skills should be a high priority for all government institutions and other providers of care and protection. This includes faith-based and community-based organizations funded by government agencies.

All programs, policies, and practices that serve communities of color should reflect this priority. In her excellent book, *Post Traumatic Slave Syndrome: America's Legacy of Enduring Injury and Healing,* Dr. Joy Degruy writes, "The legacy of trauma is reflected in many of our behaviors and our beliefs; behaviors and beliefs that at one time were necessary to adopt in order to survive, yet today serve to undermine our ability to be successful." Culturally proficient training is needed to help all service providers and child welfare professionals view all domains of life from a healing-focused perspective focused on people's potential instead of a deficit-based perspective focused on their deficiencies. They should always seek to understand how past traumas impact the current attitudes and behaviors of a family or community. They should make a deliberate effort to discard prior assumptions and engage in all discussions, treatment decisions, and other interactions with goodwill.

We can begin to achieve this goal early on, when children get their first glimpse of their place in history. There's a huge need to more accurately and comprehensively teach in our schools the rich history of the African American and Latino experience, which has largely been omitted from our textbooks. When we have a more informed and balanced perspective of the positive contributions of African Americans and the oppressive racism they have suffered, I believe we will be more motivated to challenge the implicit biases of our formal systems that oppress African Americans and Latinos.

The Reverend Jesse Jackson with the author at a Virginia Clay/Unity Care Golf Classic.

CHAPTER 11

BATTLES ON THE HOMEFRONT

After my parents' divorce when I was ten, my father wasn't much involved in my life. My mom always used to say, "Learn from your parents' mistakes." I didn't want to make that same mistake with my marriage or my children. Charlene and I went on date nights and did other things, and I took advantage of every opportunity to be present for the sports, church, and school activities of my children.

My mom had always made sure that my sister, brother, and I played every sport possible. I followed that model with my children. They all started playing basketball, baseball, football, softball, and soccer as soon as they were able to run. I stepped forward and coached both of my boys' teams in Pop Warner football and basketball pretty much all the way through elementary school and middle school.

Our teams did pretty well most of the time. For instance, André Jr.'s eighth grade basketball team won the state championship in its league. Aaron's eighth grade Pop Warner baseball team won the sec-

tional title and earned a trip to Florida for the national championship. Ariana, Daddy's baby girl, played some sports when she was younger, but as she grew, she took more interest in the arts.

Growing up, I envied my friends who took vacations with their families. When I became a father, I made it a point to give my children these types of experiences. The five of us went skiing at Tahoe, took trips to family reunions, and did other things.

President Barack Obama and the author. Taken at the home of John and Sandy Thompson in Silicon Valley. John later became chairman of the board of Microsoft.

Fighting for Aaron

One day in 2003, when my younger son Aaron was in the third grade, I got a call from his teacher. "Mr. Chapman," she said, "I'm calling to let you know that we're going to have a SST[14] meeting of all of Aaron's teachers, the school psychologist, and the principal to create a behavioral plan for your son."

After recovering from my shock, I said, "This is the first I've heard of any behavioral problems with Aaron. We're not going to have any meeting of that sort until my wife and I personally meet with you and the principal." She objected, so I called the principal. He agreed to meet with the teacher, Charlene, and me prior to the SST.

At the meeting, the teacher recited the charges against Aaron: "He is very aggressive; he pushes other kids off the computer so he can use it; he bullies his way to the front of the line; he takes the basketball away from other kids at recess; if they're not playing fast enough, he takes the ball and shoots for them."

I said, "How many other African American kids do you have in your class?"

"None," she answered.

"Well then," I continued, "let's back up and look at the situation. You first have to understand something. Most of the children in Aaron's class are either Indo-Americans or Asian. It's my experience that those children are more passive. I teach my son as a young African American male to be assertive because society knocks these kids down. By labeling his assertiveness as aggressiveness, you're putting his behaviors in a negative light, which means you're restricting his strengths and natural abilities. I don't appreciate your describing my son with that type of deficit-based terminology. It's your job as the teacher to manage your classroom and recognize the brilliance of every student, so all the children are working together."

The teacher was obviously uncomfortable with the tenor of the conversation, but I pressed on. "Second, and I don't mean this disrespectfully, you are in your mid-twenties and Caucasian, and unfortunately, Aaron's image of you is what he sees on TV. If you were in your sixties, he would view you more as a grandmother figure, and his attitude and behavior would be entirely different. So, we need to think differently about what terminology you use and how you engage my son."

We spent the rest of the meeting developing a plan of action that included an award system. When Aaron did well in school, the teacher said she would put stars on a card that he would bring home, so Charlene and I could reinforce his positive behaviors. All of us agreed to focus on teaching Aaron how to be more patient. His teacher promised to do a better job of managing the usage of the computers, so every child got his fair share of time.

Finally, we discussed how she needed to adjust her teaching style. For example, instead of directly criticizing Aaron if he answered a question out of turn, she would say something like, "That's great, Aaron, but let Lee give his

[14] The purpose of an SST (Student Study Team) meeting is to design a support system for students having difficulty in the regular classroom. The SST usually consists of the parent (s), a teacher, an administrator, and one or more support personnel from the school.

answer first, and then you can give yours." We also talked about Aaron's innate leadership skills. She agreed to look for ways to leverage them, such as putting him at the front of the line more often.

The rest of the school year went fine, but after it ended, I didn't see this teacher for two years. Then, at the beginning of Aaron's fifth grade year of school and Ariana's third, she came running up to me at an open house: "Mr. Chapman! Mr. Chapman!" I greeted her and asked her why I hadn't seen her around the school for a while.

"My husband got a job in Los Angeles," she explained, "and I taught for two years in the Los Angeles County School System. Now we've moved back here, and I'm teaching third grade again. But I have to tell you that the conversation we had that day in my classroom with the principal was a life changer for me. I didn't fully understand what you were saying at the time, and I admit it made me upset at first. But in the LA school system, I had a lot of African American students in my class, and you opened my eyes to how I should better engage with them. I just want you to know how much I appreciate your being honest with me, and I would love to have your daughter in my third grade class."

This is just an example of where my pushing back and fighting for greater cultural understanding and humility not only helped the teacher, it probably saved my child's life. If we had agreed to participate in an SST meeting with all of Aaron's teachers, the school psychologist and the principal almost certainly would have prescribed medication, requested an Individualized Education Plan (IEP), and instituted various restrictions to mitigate Aaron's "aggressive" behaviors. The school system would have documented these "problems" and the remedial actions taken in his CUM file.[15] Anyone accessing that file, for years to come, would regard what was written there as the "truth."

All children are unique individuals. In addition to having varying innate characteristics and personalities, they are profoundly shaped by their different cultural backgrounds, family customs, beliefs, circumstances, and other factors. We need to take these differences into account and value their uniqueness when teaching and parenting them. The battles for the welfare of our children are waged in every school and in every home every day. In many of these battles, children unfortunately do not have someone advocating and pushing back on our educational systems at every step along the way. We, as a community, need to have advocates in our schools to prevent the kind of mistakes that might have taken my son down a damaging path. Our institutions and professionals that deliver services need to have greater cultural proficiency.

---

[15] A cumulative file (CUM file) must be kept for every student in California's public schools, according to state law. These records usually begin in first grade and are mailed directly from a child's old school to his or her new ones, until graduation. From such a file, it is possible to obtain an overall view of the child's academic and behavioral progress.

Fighting for My Marriage

In spite of my busyness, I also devoted quite a lot of time to my marriage. As our children grew, however, Charlene seemed to grow apart from me and them. I could tell things weren't going well. We discussed our relationship and read books about how to have a healthy marriage. Over time, however, it became clearer and clearer that we were simply growing in different directions.

Thinking back, I'm sure I could have done some things differently. It takes two committed individuals to make a marriage. In spite of my best efforts, by 2005 our relationship was in critical condition. I considered filing for divorce, but for the sake of our children, I held off. I didn't believe in divorce, so I tried to work through our problems with additional commitment and counseling.

However, by 2009 it became clear that our marriage wasn't going to work. At this point, the kids were older and more capable of dealing with a family breakup, so I filed for divorce. Charlene took Ariana and André Jr.; Aaron stayed with me. It was painful. The man who had dedicated his life to putting families together was now head of a family that was breaking apart.

In addition to the emotional strains, we were in the middle of the worst economy since the Great Recession. Unity Care struggled to keep the doors open. I was right up against my personal breaking point.

As the agency leader, I couldn't afford to show my brokenness. I would take quiet moments out of the day, close my office door, and listen to my favorite song, "God Favored Me." I have a picture over my desk of a man with armor and a shield. The caption says, "No weapon formed against you shall prosper." That's a quote from Isaiah 57:14, and it's my constant motivator.

I turned to my family and friends for support. My father, who lives in San Jose, helped with the kids, and my mom, who lives in Fremont, cooked a week's worth of dinners for us, which I picked up after church on Sundays. It truly took constant prayer and a broad support system to get through this very difficult time.

Through it all, Unity Care continued to grow. Almost before I realized it, we had a staff of 150 dedicated people and an annual budget of more than $8 million. More important than the growth of our organization, however, was the growth of our positive influence in the lives of kids and families.

I keep this poster on my wall.

CHAPTER 12

BUILDING A VILLAGE

A 2015 study in Santa Clara County showed that 14.9 percent of African American and 20.8 percent of Hispanic/Latino students were dropping out of high school each year, compared to 4.5 percent of white students and only 3.1 percent of Asian American students.[16] Young people who do not complete high school are more likely to struggle with employment, live in poverty, be dependent on welfare benefits, have poor physical and mental health, and engage in criminal activity than those with higher education levels. Something needed to be done.

When people think about improving education, they generally talk about things like curriculum development, improving test scores, lengthening the school year, putting more emphasis on summer school, focusing on teacher development, and so on. They don't talk about supporting families and mitigating risk factors due to poverty, homelessness, or chronic health problems. I think this is because they don't know how to tackle these societal issues, so they restrict their focus to the schools.

I always tell people that although poverty can be a contributing factor to poor academic achievement, it should never be used as an excuse. Plenty of kids born into poverty grow up to accomplish great things. Rather, I am convinced that a primary cause of this poor performance is the failure of schools to address the impact of adverse childhood experiences (ACEs) in underserved communities. The only way to deal with these sources of trauma is to wrestle with them in the trenches, in strong collaboration with communities, systems partners, teachers, and administrators. We'll never solve our educational problems until our school systems see themselves as integral parts of the communities they serve. They need to recognize that they are contributors to this trauma, and they also must recognize that they can be healers of this trauma.

Many economic, social, and institutional factors impact children's health and well-being and their ultimate success in school. They include poverty and economic self-sufficiency, hunger and food insecurity, housing and neighborhood

[16] http://www.kidsdata.org/topic/106/highschooldropouts-race/table#fmt=193&loc=59&tf=84& ch=7,11,726,85,10,72,9,73&sortColumnId=0&sortType=asc

conditions, homelessness, discrimination, and immigration. Children do not leave their family's burdens at the door when they arrive at school. While teachers, administrators, and other staff strive to meet the needs that students bring to school, shrinking financial resources, larger class sizes, and reductions in the number of counselors and school nurses make it increasingly difficult for schools to address all of these issues.

There is a great deal of literature supporting the need for a stronger relationship between education and public child serving systems, so both can achieve their distinct mandates. Success in learning is closely tied to a child's emotional well-being and the self-sufficiency and stability of the child's family. Partnerships between the schools, mental health departments, probation officers, social service agencies, and community-based organizations are needed to serve the broader needs of families and communities. The goal should be to connect families with needed resources, supports, and services in advance, before severe crises arise that adversely impact a child's educational trajectory.

At Unity Care, we began to think about developing a program that would provide appropriate resources and supports for students from underserved communities. When children from families with resources are struggling in schools, their families often will send them to a private learning center, like Sylvan, Kumon, or Mathnasium, or they may arrange for them to have private tutoring or counseling. Most families in underserved communities don't have the resources to acquire this type of specialized support, so they do nothing. We wanted to rectify this inequity.

A Community-Based Educational Model

As part of our seven-month planning process, and in partnership with the community and the county, we conducted extensive research to learn what other communities across the country were doing to combat this educational crisis in underserved communities. We were most impressed with the UCLA Learning Model, with its three-tier framework. Level 1 focuses on increasing students' engagement with the schools; Level 2 focuses on providing counseling and other supportive services in the schools; and Level 3 focuses on mitigating substance abuse, domestic violence, and other risk factors in the families of the children.

We studied both school-based and community-based programs. The problem with school-based programs, in our opinion, was that they generally have little to no connection to the homes of the students. The community-based programs, on the other hand, are generally disconnected from the schools. We saw the need to replace this fragmented, disconnected approach with a seamless, comprehensive support system across all tiers from the home to the classroom.

If you take your car to a dealership to have the oil changed, the brakes checked, some body work done, the seatbelt fixed, and a strange sound in the engine investigated, you only need to talk with one person: the service representative. But with issues relating to our school aged kids, parents have to talk to different teachers about the various subjects, a counselor about behavioral and emotional issues, the principal about discipline issues, and maybe even the coach about athletic issues. It's easy for parents to get overwhelmed, and it's difficult for them to get a clear, overall picture of where things stand.

Out of our research emerged a vision for a community-based model that was very different from the traditional school-based approach. Our studies convinced us that youths are most exposed to the risks of trauma in their homes, neighborhoods, and schools. So, we decided to turn the educational pyramid upside down and focus more services on where students lived. We set out to build a model that integrated home and school with a continuum of services and open communications.

Nationwide, our country spends billions of dollars on educational reform efforts, with 99 percent of those reforms taking place at the school. The schools are doing their best, but the system is failing the kids. Schools are not addressing problems at their source, which is usually in children's homes and neighborhoods. The great majority of counselors and mental health staff who work in the schools are competent, dedicated professionals, but their working hours and freedom of movement are restricted. School staff are not able to go into the homes of kids and work with their families between 3:00 p.m. and 7:00 p.m., which is when they could have the biggest impact.

Teachers and administrators often complain that parents are not engaged. As evidence, they point to poor attendance at parent-teacher events and the failure to return teachers' phone calls. But many parents, especially those who themselves struggled in school, can feel intimidated and disempowered when they receive calls or meeting requests from teachers and administrators. Furthermore, parents who work are often unable to come to the school during the day without jeopardizing their jobs.

School teachers and administrators who fail to understand these dynamics may complain about parents' lack of engagement. But when it comes to attending their child's art show or the school's football or basketball games on Friday nights, these same parents can be really engaged!

We realized that we needed to help schools redefine "engagement." Instead of focusing on how many times parents come to the school, or how involved they are with school activities, we decided to focus on how fully parents were involved in their child's academic success at home.

Planning Imani Village

After numerous meetings with community and county officials, using the grant we received from the county, we launched our initiative. Our community partners suggested the name Imani Village. In Swahili, "Imani" means faith. We wanted to restore faith in our children and their abilities. Our strategy revolved around serving children and families in these communities out of village hubs in schools and churches.

Imani Village had the following five major goals for middle and high school youths and their families:

1. Reduce school suspensions and expulsions

2. Improve academic achievement

3. Promote parent involvement and participation in their child's education

4. Enhance social emotional well-being of students and family members

5. Increase access to resources for families facing multiple significant risk factors

We expanded the UCLA learning model by incorporating intensive, culturally proficient family and child supports, with the goal of mitigating and reducing risk factors caused by poverty and systemic biases. Our desire was to enable youths and families to move fluidly between the tiers of services listed below, so they could access the services that best fit their needs.

Tier 1 Services: Universal interventions, including assessments, student self-evaluations, tutoring, advocacy service, and other prevention-oriented activities, such as parent empowerment sessions, field trips, and guest motivational speakers.

Tier 2 Services: Educational, mental health, and substance abuse prevention services. During school hours, our staff would help students develop emotional self-management and social skills to improve their classroom behaviors and functioning. After school, staff would be available to help students and their families with challenges unrelated to school.

Tier 3 Services: Intensive therapeutic interventions, including crisis intervention, therapeutic behavioral services, individual and family therapy, or case management. These services were intended to address any severe academic, behavioral, and social-emotional risk factors that may be impeding a student's success. To promote maximum success for youths, we would offer these services at settings desired by the family. When appropriate, we would engage the community and other stakeholders.

This model gave us a framework for providing culturally proficient wraparound services for educational success. From our background in foster care, we knew that if a child is living at home in an environment of domestic violence, extreme poverty, neighborhood crime, substance abuse, or other adverse childhood experiences (ACEs), even the best supportive services at school are unlikely to result in academic success.[17] Education had always been one of Unity Care's five pillars, so Imani Village was a natural outgrowth of our foster care program.

Launching Imani Village

We opened our first Imani Village Hub at Oak Grove High School in San Jose in August 2014. It was an immediate success. Within four months, we opened five more village hubs in middle schools, plus two village hubs that operated out of community churches.

Students came into the village hubs throughout the day for support and counseling related to academic and family issues. (Our church programs operated in the evenings.) Every student referred to the Imani Village program received an in-home visit from our academic counselors. This included a universal assessment to evaluate both the academic needs of the student and the well-being needs of the student's family. Families in need of well-being support were immediately connected to our Tier 3 clinical teams and case managers.

We developed a comprehensive plan that addressed all aspects of a student's circumstances, including any family struggles. If a youth was failing in science and math, for example, in addition to arranging for tutoring, we might also help the family deal with a grandmother who was struggling with diabetes and a parent who was out of work. We provided a continuum of educational and counseling support across the board. Our approach recognized that the academic issues were most often the visible symptoms of adverse challenges at home.

We conducted an academic assessment and created an individual success plan for each student in the program, taking into account the youth's needs and the state's standards. We also administered tests to determine the learning style of each student. Students who are good test takers generally do well in school. The visual learners, however, have a more difficult time. Our tutoring incorporated hands-on teaching methods that tapped into the visual side of children's brains.

Imani Village worked collaboratively with the schools and the community. If a student came to school looking disheveled, or if a mom didn't return a teacher's phone calls, the schools often referred the matter to us rather than call child protective services. We'd drive to the student's home, knock on the door, and ask the parent if he or she would like to talk about the benefits of our program.

In most schools, parents only hear from the school when their child is in trouble, and they only go to the school when called in to discuss a behavioral issue. This deficit-based approach intimidates families and causes them to feel uncomfortable around the schools. In many cases, it retraumatizes the parents.

---

[17] Our approach was supported by a collaborative study of more than 17,000 members of health maintenance organization (HMOs) conducted by the Centers for Disease Control and Prevention and Kaiser Permanente's Health Appraisal Clinic. https://www.cdc.gov/violenceprevention/acestudy/about.html

Imani Village Cultural Day attended by more than 500 teachers and students

We wanted Imani Village to create a welcoming environment, so we regularly called parents to give them positive reports, and we opened cafés for parents in the evenings. We spoke the school's language to the parents, and the parents' language to the schools. If a child was in danger of suspension or expulsion, we advocated for that child and brought a cultural and linguistic perspective to the conversation.

Encouraging Feedback

School administrators, teachers, and counselors praised the program. Most schools in underserved communities have no more than one or two counselors for the thousands of students enrolled, and these counselors simply don't have the time or the mandate to delve into issues outside of school. Most teachers don't have time to deal with behavioral and other personal issues in addition to fulfilling their teaching responsibilities. The supportive resources Imani Village brings to the campus leverage the effectiveness of teachers and counselors.

We constantly talked to students about going to college, and we reassured them that they could accomplish anything they set their minds to. Academic averages improved whole grade points. Behavioral problems decreased, and the number of names on the school's expulsion watch list dramatically declined. Parents started talking about higher education for all of their kids, even in families where no one had ever gone to college.

We received considerable positive feedback from families. One grandmother said, "I referred my grandson to Imani Village because of his low academic performance, low confidence level, and poor peer selection. He now frequently participates in the tutoring services and receives mentoring from an Imani Village team member. As a result of his involvement in Imani Village, his grades have improved from failing to above average. Most notably, he was selected to serve as the president for the BSU (Black Student Union). I am very thankful for my grandson's improvements and the impact Imani Village is having in his life."

Our after-school parent workshops and African American and Latino history days were well attended. "We've never had so many parents come to school for anything!" an administrator exclaimed to me after one workshop.

A middle school counselor wrote, "One of our students had frequent visits to the office for disciplinary infractions. He was suspended from school six times last year. Our school staff referred the student to Imani Village. Within a short period of time, our staff noticed improvement in his behavior. He meets with the Imani Village team twice a week. During the last grading period, the majority of his grades improved from Ds and Fs to Cs. His disciplinary referrals to the office declined tremendously, and he hasn't received an out-of-school suspension this year. Our school staff credited the work and services provided by Imani Village for helping this student make continuous improvements."

Dr. Arnetha F. Ball, Professor, Curriculum, Teacher Education & Educational Linguistics, Stanford Graduate School of Education, has selected Imani Village as a focus of her research. Dr. Teresa LaFromboise, Professor, Developmental and Psychological Sciences, Stanford Graduate School of Education, signed on to assist in the research, along with Caitlin Annand-Bacchtel and Efrain Brito, two students from Stanford's Graduate School of Education. Suddenly, we had some of the nation's leading educational authorities researching the efficacy of the Imani Village model.

Dr. Ball and her research team stated, "Imani Village is poised to become a leading service provider in Santa Clara County. They [Unity Care] are the first organization in the area to attempt to merge mental health and academic support, an integrated approach important to the holistic health of a child."

My hope is that Imani Village will become a model that other communities and states emulate.

CHAPTER 13

OPPORTUNITIES AND CHALLENGES

Back when André Jr. was in middle school, he kept bringing home a fellow named Pierre. The two guys were very good friends. Pierre loved to hang around our house, but when it got late, he'd just disappear.

One day, I talked with Pierre and found out that he was living in a foster care treatment home. His father was out of the picture and his mom was in jail. I invited him to live with us during his eighth grade year. I also invited him to play on the basketball team I coached. He readily accepted both offers.

Things went well for Pierre that school year. When his mom got out of jail in the middle of his ninth grade year, he went back to live with her. A short time later, his mom hit hard times and Pierre went to live with a friend in another city. I kept up with him while he was in high school by occasionally going to his basketball games, and sometimes he'd spend weekends at our house with André Jr. Upon graduation from high school, André Jr. attended college at UCLA, and Pierre enrolled at a junior college.

I didn't see much of him for quite a while after that, until one day there was a knock on my door. It was Pierre. Beside him stood a young girl holding a newborn baby. A U-Haul truck was parked in our driveway. The look on Pierre's face told me he was desperate.

"I'll take you in," I said to Pierre, "but I can't take care of your baby and your girlfriend. They need to go live with the mom's family."

Pierre agreed and moved in with me. In addition to requiring that he go to school, I put him in a very aggressive technology immersion program called "YearUp." For the first six months he learned technology and job training, and for the second six months he interned with a technology company. When he finished this one-year program, Pierre went to work for Google. As I write this, he's living on his own, raising his daughter as a single dad, and making excellent money in IT sales while finishing school. This is just one example of how a kid can turn his life around when you give him love, support, and guidance. We all have the ability to give back. It's not necessary to work full-time in a foster care organization to impact kids' lives.

I have always sub-scribed to my mother's philosophy that sports are one of the best ways to teach kids about teamwork, discipline, and dealing with the triumphs and trials of life. Unstructured time is one of biggest enemies that kids face, so I kept my kids plenty busy.

In addition to excelling at basketball, André Jr. was on the 4x100-meter relay

Pierre and his daughter, Khaliah

team that set his high school's record. Upon graduation with a 3.4 academic average, he earned a track scholarship to UCLA.

His younger brother, Aaron, excelled at football and track. Even though a torn ACL caused him to miss most of the football season during his junior and senior years, he recovered enough in the spring of his senior year to help his 4x100-meter relay team break the school record his brother had helped set two years before. He maintained a 3.0 academic average and was recruited to play football for the University of Washington.

Ariana went to a Christian middle school and then to a public high school. The youngest child, and the only girl in our family, she seemed to be most impacted by the divorce. After playing volleyball and basketball during her freshman year, she discovered hip-hop dance and pursued it with a passion, while furthering her education.

At André Jr.'s graduation from UCLA.
From left: Aaron, André Jr., Ariana, the author

Pursuing Destiny

In March of 2010, I got a call from my good friend, Carl Agers. "Tonight's the last night of the Cinequest Film Festival. My wife Sheri plans to bring along a girlfriend of hers. Why don't you join us? I think you'll enjoy meeting her."

The Cinequest Film Festival in San Jose is one of the biggest in the world, but I had just arrived home and I was dead tired. "I appreciate the invitation, Carl," I said. "Maybe another time." But Carl kept insisting, so I changed clothes and joined the three of them at the after-cinema festivities.

Sheri's friend, Teresa Arriola, really impressed me. Two weeks later, we met for dinner. We again had a very enjoyable evening, but after that I got busy with my kids, my work, and life's challenges, so we lost touch.

Two years went by. One day, my fraternity brother, Cedric Martin, called. "Hey, André, there's a lady who sings at our church. She's really nice. I think you should meet her." I brushed his suggestion aside, but a few days later he again said, "This lady says she knows you, André. She's the worship singer in our church and she also sings professionally. I think you'd like her."

"I don't know any lady who sings in a church," I insisted. But Cedric kept telling me about this fabulous lady, until I finally realized that I did know her. She was the same Teresa I had met at the film festival with the Agers. I told Cedric that I'd be happy to go out with her.

Cedric arranged it, and the following Friday night I took Teresa to dinner. As we were chatting away and having a good time, a text came in on my cell phone from Carl Agers. "Tomorrow is the last night of the Cinequest Film Festival. Sheri and I are going. Do you want me to get you a ticket?"

I texted back: "Put me down for two." When Teresa and I showed up the following night, Carl and Sheri were shocked...and delighted! After that, Teresa and I saw a lot of each other, and we've since made attending the last night of the Cinequest Film Festival an annual tradition. On December 27, 2014, she accepted my proposal of marriage.

Teresa Arriola and the author

Coming Full Circle

Around this time, the Reverend Horacio Jones, the pastor of my church, called and asked if I'd be willing to speak to the congregation about the importance of pursuing one's passion. He wanted me to share how I chose to leave the business world and lead a non-profit foster care ministry. I thought, "What remarkable timing! God has brought things full circle. This very pastor's words, many years before, had prompted my decision."

When I spoke to the congregation, I told them that I still remembered the Sunday when Pastor Jones challenged us with the question, "Are you walking in faith, or are you walking in the ways of the world?" I then turned and looked at Pastor Jones. "When you said those words, I felt you were looking straight at me. God used that question to change my life. Once I took the first steps, He opened door after door. He supplied all my needs, and He went before me into every battle. It's an amazing thing to experience the faithfulness of God."

After my talk, Pastor Jones said to me in front of the congregation, "Your words really spoke to me today. God used them to remind me that there's something I've been avoiding that I need to step out in faith and do."

I was really touched by his comment. His words had initially helped me step out in faith, and now my words were helping him do the same.

YouthLive! Is Alive and Well

On April 25, 2015, I again found myself looking out at hundreds of people seated at banquet tables that filled the grand ballroom of the San Jose Fairmont Hotel. The occasion was Unity Care's fourth annual YouthLive! banquet. It was at this same event two years before that Makel Ali had given his stirring testimony about

how Unity Care had transformed his life. Our keynote speaker on this night was Leigh Anne Tuohy, the heroine of the bestselling book and smash hit movie, *The Blind Side*.

Leigh Anne began her talk with a side-splitting account of her family's trip to the Academy Awards ceremony in Hollywood, where *The Blind Side* competed for best picture, and Sandra Bullock, the star of

Spencer Christian of ABC News, Leigh Anne Tuohy, and the author at YouthLive! 2015

the movie, was a nominee for best actress. It was the first time her family had ever been to California, Leigh Anne explained, and actually one of the few times they had ever been out of Memphis. To the roars of the crowd, she described how her family's Southern-style behaviors created near havoc in Tinseltown. "They'll never invite us back!" she joked.

After the laughter had died down, Leigh Anne told the story about how she and her family brought Michael Oher, a six-foot, six-inch, 350-pound African American youth, into their home and eventually adopted him as their own son. "It has been a journey that we never expected...I promise to you with every fiber of my body," said Leigh Anne. "I did not grab the to-do list one morning and say, 'Drive down the street, find a large black boy, and adopt him and make him a famous football player.' I wish I was that smart, but I did not do that. I did not. This was just one of those God-driven moments."

Leigh Anne went on to talk about how the movie was actually very accurate. "We were driving down the street, just like the movie showed," she continued. "I do not like to cook...so, on the Wednesday before Thanksgiving we were going for breakfast. I tell everybody in my house, when I pick the restaurant, load the family in the car, drive them there, and pay for the food, that's a home cooked meal.

"So, we were going for a home cooked breakfast, and we drove by Michael. As a mother, every warning bell in my head went off, because here was this kid in a lily-white neighborhood, inappropriately dressed for the weather on a holiday. I just knew something wasn't right. So, I said to my husband, 'Turn around!' He dutifully obeyed — he's very coachable — and we pulled up next to Michael."

Across the banquet hall, I could see husbands and wives laughing at Leigh Anne's remark about her husband being "coachable." Leigh Anne continued: "I looked at Michael and said, 'Hey, I'm Leigh Anne Tuohy, and my two kids go to school with you.' He wouldn't look at me; he wouldn't talk to me; he wanted nothing to do with that entire moment that was happening. And I said, 'Well, what are you doing here?' No answer. I said, 'You know, school's closed.' No answer. And I said, 'Okay, here's the deal. I'm not leaving, and you're not staying. So, we need to converse. You speak; I speak; that's called a conversation. So, let's have one of those and figure this out.' Michael eventually allowed us to take him to a bus stop."

Nobody Cares

By this time, people in the audience were sitting on the edge of their seats. Leigh Anne continued: "The next Monday morning I was at the expensive private Christian school that Michael and my two kids attended. I went around talking to teacher after teacher: 'Tell me something about Michael Oher.' 'Who?' they said. Not one of the teachers I asked knew anything about him. I asked them, 'How in the world can you miss a six-foot, six-inch, 350-pound black kid in a lily-white school?'

"After five or six of these responses, I was fed up. I marched straight to the principal's office and said, 'Here's the deal: I want you to open the checkbook and reimburse my tuition for my two kids that are here, because you have a bunch of idiots teaching my children. There is a six-foot, six-inch, 350-pound black kid running around here, and they don't know who he is!'"

More laughter; Leigh Anne continued. "To this day, the principal's response haunts me. He looked at me and said, 'Leigh Anne, don't get involved. Don't get involved. This isn't a project. Don't get involved. He's not going to make it.'

"I wasn't looking for a third kid," Leigh Ann assured the audience. "Trust me! I don't even like my two biological kids." After the chuckles from the audience died down, Leigh Anne resumed.

"Michael eventually allowed us to take him shopping for a rugby shirt. Afterwards, when we dropped him off at a bus stop, I realized how alone in the world he was. If Michael had had a major heart attack on the sidewalk, not a single, solitary person in this world would have cared, because society deemed my son 100 percent valueless. One hundred percent! Nobody cared about Michael Oher. Nobody!"

Silence fell over the room, as Leigh Anne made eye contact with the members of the audience. After several seconds, she continued. "In the next twenty-four hours, most of us will walk or drive by somebody who will be holding a sign at the corner, or they'll be cleaning the office that you work in, or they'll be doing lawn service when you pull up. And we'll look at them, and we'll size them up; we'll pigeonhole them and put them in a spot. And we go, 'Hmm, they smell horrible. Where did they get those shoes they got on? They need a shirt. I wonder when's the last time they washed their hair.'

"That's pretty much what they said about my son, Michael," Leigh Anne continued. "All we did was turn our car around. We turned our car around and offered this young man hope and love and opportunity. We changed his life. We changed his life! And you'll go, 'Oh, I can't do that. You took a risk. You took this big black kid into your house, and you had a daughter the same age. Are you crazy? Oh my gosh, what were you thinking?'

"But we all take risks. There's not a soul in this room who, if you had to cross a bridge to come here tonight, first put your car in park and got out, inspected that bridge and said, 'Yep, this bridge is going to hold us.' No! Tires blow up, bridges fall in, and people die—we all take risks!"

From the Streets to Stadiums

Leigh Anne paused to let her words sink in before continuing. "Michael Oher almost fell through the cracks, but he became a star NFL football player with the Carolina Panthers. If someone who is such an obvious success story as Michael Oher almost falls through the cracks, can you imagine who actually does get left behind? Can you imagine? It could be the kid that discovers the cure for cancer, the next outstanding policeman, the next great attorney, the next top sales rep... and all they need is a chance. They just need a chance. They need someone to believe in them. They just need someone to offer them help, love, and opportunity.

My kid, Michael Oher, is the starting left tackle for the Carolina Panthers, a contributing member of society, and for all practical purposes he should be dead. He was tapped to be a gang bodyguard in Memphis, Tennessee. The life expectancy of one is eighteen to twenty-four months, three years if you're lucky. He was six-feet, six-inches tall when he was only in like the eighth grade, and every gang in the city knew about him. He almost fell through the cracks. And all we did was turn our car around.

"So, you ask what you can do. You sit there and you say, 'Well, I'm just one little person in this world. I don't know if I can make a difference. Guys, we were Michael Oher's whole world. And if you got up this morning, and you got dressed, and you're sitting here, and you're listening to me, then you were born with the ability to make a difference in someone's life. Yes, you were." The audience applauded; many wiped away tears.

Leigh Anne continued: "You know, I listened to André earlier, and he said Unity Care started off with one child, one house. And it's about the power of one. We were the ones who benefited from having Michael in our house. We were the ones who gained. We learned about being a family; we learned about giving unconditionally. Giving will change your life. It will change your life!

"And that is what Unity Care is doing. That is what they are providing. There's no kid in this world who dreams of being in foster care. It's a flawed, horrible system. These kids don't ask to be there. But you know the beauty of it: the members of foster families don't have to match. And if there's not somebody in your social circle that doesn't look like you, shame on you! It's about loving someone who doesn't look like you.

"You can do something. Do something today that you didn't do yesterday. Doing nothing is not an option. Get out of your comfort zone. Nothing exciting happens in your comfort zone. If you want to know what to do, come see André or any of these other board members. They'll give you a list. This group and these kids are worth the effort!"

As Leigh Anne said these concluding words, everyone in the room rose and gave her a standing ovation. I've reprinted significant portions of her moving presentation because they sum up my sentiments and the theme of this book so well.

CHAPTER 14

A WHOLE NEW LEVEL

After our YouthLive! event, we kicked off our annual Summer of Learning program, which exposes youths to a host of outdoor summer activities that families with resources typically enjoy. From June through August, we took more than four hundred youths on tours of colleges, trips to amusement parks, horseback rides, camping excursions to Yosemite National Park, and other outings.

Summer of Learning field trip on the beach in Carmel, California

As we entered the fall, everything was on an upward swing. We were in the midst of rolling out our five-year strategic plan, and I was spending a great deal of time focusing on systematic changes in foster care at the county, state, and federal levels. At the same time, we were bursting at the seams trying to keep up with the high demands of our youth and families. We were seeing nearly a double-digit increase in the number of youths aging out of foster care, and that was creating a pressing need for housing and mental health services. On top of that, a large percentage of families in our educational and community-based programs were struggling with housing, unemployment, substance use, and mental health challenges.

We started a few new programs in our attempt to keep up with the increased demands, but it soon became evident that we needed to look internally at how we could enhance our organizational capacity. The growing complexity and needs of Unity Care were crying out for someone with outstanding operational qualities and experience in the field, so I decided to reach out to a well-respected colleague named Sheila Mitchell.

I had met Sheila in 2003, when she was hired as the county's Chief Probation Officer, with responsibilities for overseeing the Juvenile and Adult Probation Department. Over the years, she had become one of the most sought-out leaders in the country, with a reputation as an extraordinary agent of positive change. When I contacted Sheila, she was living in Atlanta and about to step into an important position as Chief County Director of Albemarle County, Virginia, near Charlottesville.

During more than a week, Sheila and I had several phone conversations about Unity Care's needs and challenges. Then, I asked her if she would consider becoming our Chief Operating Officer. She called me back after considerable thought and prayer and said "Yes." Sheila's acceptance of my offer tangibly illustrated the extent of her love for Unity Care and the youths and families we serve.

At the next meeting of Unity Care's board of directors, which was also attended by several highly respected community leaders and executives of large organizations, my proposal that Unity Care hire Sheila Mitchell to be our Chief Operating Officer was unanimously approved. We spent a large portion of the meeting restructuring the organization with Sheila as the COO and several respected people from the community serving on an oversight board. We developed an organizational restructuring plan of improvement and shared it with our staff, the community, and the county.

Gold Refined by Fire

In April, more than four hundred guests came out for our annual YouthLive! event. We awarded our Community Champion Award to William J. Del Biaggio, chairman of Heritage Bank in Silicon Valley, who had been a long-time supporter and source of inspiration. Our youth speaker for the evening was Elizabeth Cartagena, a 21-year-old former foster youth and alumna of our transitional housing program. She shared the captivating story about her journey through the foster care experience and the lifesaving benefits she received through our transitional housing program. This was a powerful reminder of the need for housing and a helpful confirmation of our strategic direction.

"Just know that we are gold," said Elizabeth, speaking directly to the youths who were present. "We've been through the fire. This life is preparing you for great things, but you have to go through the fire to get there. History's most influential people have had to face severe hardships."

Elizabeth's speech about her trials really spoke to me. We were experiencing the same kinds of trials as an organization. After her talk, many individuals offered Elizabeth employment opportunities, and some offered to help her fulfill her dream of applying to Santa Clara University. Unity Care raised more than $150,000 that evening, which we dedicated to improving the lives of the more than 6,000 children and families we were serving each year in foster care and beyond.

The author, Elizabeth Cartagena, and Bill J. Del Biaggio at YouthLive!

An Uplifting Encounter

After the YouthLive! gala, I was feeling mentally and physically exhausted from the daily battles with the system on behalf of youths and the organization. With Sheila on board to run the daily operations of the agency, for the first time in many years, I had the freedom to take a vacation. Teresa and I moved our wedding date up from July to May and made plans for a ten-day honeymoon in Italy.

On May 18, the day before our wedding, I felt physically and emotionally exhausted. I was even wondering if it was time for me to move on to something different. I cried out to God to give me some guidance. What are you trying to tell me, Lord? Is it time for someone else to take over the reins at Unity Care? Is this as far as you want me to take the organization?

As I was leaving my office to start my two-week marriage vacation, I noticed a young woman across the railroad tracks that run behind Unity Care's main offices. I immediately recognized her as Porshia. She had graduated from our program fifteen years before, and I hadn't seen her since. Considering the thousands and thousands of youths I had interacted with over the intervening years, it was rather miraculous that I instantly recognized her and remembered her name. I called out to Porshia, and she came running over.

"I've been looking for you for months," she exclaimed, giving me a big hug. "It's really good to see you. What's been going on?"

With tears in her eyes, Porshia explained that she had been homeless for several months. She said she was now living in her truck with her three kids, who were in danger of being taken away. Although she had a full-time job at Home Depot, she didn't earn enough to support herself and her three daughters. I took her to our office and connected her with staff who could help her get back on her feet.

I had a strong sense that this extraordinary encounter was God's answer to my cry for guidance. "You are doing valuable work," He seemed to be telling me. "In this storm that has been raging around you, I have never left you. I am using these trials to prepare you and Unity Care for even greater work."

These thoughts reminded me of Elizabeth Cartagena's speech at YouthLive! They made me realize once again that even when we caregivers are mired deep in problems, the difficulties that accost youths and families don't let up. Every day, kids come in who need love and support. Someone has to be there for them. Unity Care offers hope to those who otherwise would have no hope. I humbly rededicated myself to our awesome mission.

Before leaving my office, I took a few minutes to write the following email to the staff:

> Message to All Staff & Board:
>
> To my amazing team of Unity Care employees: (We are all so blessed)
>
> I truly appreciate all the well-wishes and congratulations – as many of you may be aware, I am getting married (yes married) and will be on vacation for the next two weeks returning June 6th. (yes vacation)
>
> I will be unable to return emails, messages, etc. until I return. Leverage your ELT members (Steve, Wil, Deb, Gary & Sheila), and during my absence Sheila Mitchell is in charge. She's your go-to person as well as Yvette.
>
> Please continue to be the best staff doing the best work for our youth and families – remember our youth and families Depend On Us More Than You Think!!
>
> I need to share a quick story, as this just happened to me an hour ago as I was walking out of the Parkmore building thinking about all my last-minute stuff – then GOD showed up – and reminded me just how important WE are as SERVANTS to a hurting population. Our Divine purpose....
>
> I was walking out the back door across the railroad tracks and saw this lady (mid-thirties), and I immediately recognized her, as she was

one of our first girls in our group home some 17 years ago when we opened our first girls' home – house #4. I called out her name and she just ran to me with joy and gave me the biggest hug and just started weeping. I was overwhelmed, truly overwhelmed, as her name just came to me like I had seen her yesterday instead of 15+ years ago – she said she'd been looking for me – and then she took me to her truck to meet her 3 daughters – and said "this is my 2nd dad" and we spent the next 30 minutes catching up. She is in need of housing – works full-time but is homeless. I won't go into her stuff – but as I was preparing to leave, mind and body for my personal stuff – I was rocked back into being a Servant and how GOD has ordained this agency to serve those in need. Imagine if she had shown up 1 minute later we would have missed each other. WOW....

So as I leave for 2 weeks, I want to remind each of you that We all have a mighty responsibility to Be Present – Be Humble – and Be Servants – which means it's not about us, our personal agendas, our personal conflicts, our personal feelings – but it's about those we serve as we've chosen this path to be servants and give hope – give inspiration – give light and give honor – no one said it was going to be easy – but as a TEAM (Together Everyone Achieves More) there's nothing we can't accomplish...so thank YOU to each of you that consistently show up each day and labor with good intent and a heart to give back!!!!

Lift up each other each day with words of power and victory...... Remember the Power of Words:

"Watch your thoughts; they become words. Watch your words; they become actions. Watch your actions, they become habits. Watch your habits, they become character. Watch your character; it becomes your destiny." – Frank Outlaw

"Let no corrupting talk come out of your mouths, but only such as is good or building up, as fits the occasion, that it may give grace to those who hear." Matthew 12:36

"Gracious words are like a honeycomb, sweetness to the soul and health to the body." Proverbs 16:24

See everyone on June 6th!!!!

On May 19, 2016, my best friend and the love of my life, Teresa Arriola, became Mrs. André Chapman. We enjoyed a wonderful ten-day honeymoon in Italy, soaking up the rich culture and scenic beauty of Rome, Florence, and Venice. What a joyful, much needed reprieve it was from the day-to-day responsibilities of caring for Unity Care!

Mr. and Mrs. André Chapman immediately after the wedding

When Teresa and I returned from our honeymoon, the pressures of Unity Care were there to greet me. Someone created a poster with the theme "Under His Wings You Will Find Refuge." It had a scripture verse corresponding to every letter in the words "Unity Care." We often put up posters like this as reminders to keep our eyes on the Lord and trust Him to guide us through these rough waters, but this poster was especially meaningful to me. Several weeks went by before I learned that the "someone" who created it was actually my wife, Teresa.

 Unity Care

UNDER HIS WINGS YOU WILL FIND REFUGE; HIS FAITHFULNESS WILL BE YOUR SHIED. —PSALM 91:4

NO WEAPON FORMED AGAINST YOU SHALL PROSPER—ISAIAH 54:17

I CAN DO ALL THINGS THROUGH CHRIST WHO STRENGTHENS ME. —PHILLIPIANS 4:13

TRUST IN THE LORD WITH ALL YOUR HEART AND LEAN NOT ON YOUR OWN UNDERSTANDING; IN ALL YOUR WAYS ACKNOWLEDGE HIM, AND HE SHALL DIRECT YOUR PATHS —PROVERBS 3:5-6

YET IN ALL THESE THINGS WE ARE MORE THAN CONQUERORS THROUGH HIM WHO LOVED US. —ROMANS 8:37

CAST YOUR CARES ON THE LORD AND HE WILL SUSTAIN YOU; HE WILL NEVER LET THE RIGHTEOUS FALL. —PSALM 55:22

ABOVE ALL, LOVE EACH OTHER DEEPLY, BECAUSE LOVE COVERS OVER A MULTITUDE OF SINS. —1 PETER 4:8

RESTORE TO ME THE JOY OF YOUR SALVATION AND GRANT ME A WILLING SPIRIT, TO SUSTAIN ME. —PSALM 51:10

EACH OF YOU SHOULD LOOK NOT ONLY TO YOUR OWN INTERESTS, BUT ALSO TO THE INTERESTS OF OTHERS. —PHILLIPPIANS 2:4

OUR MISSION IS TO PROVIDE QUALITY YOUTH AND FAMILY PROGRAMS FOR THE PURPOSE OF CREATING HEALTHIER COMMUNITIES THROUGH LIFELONG PARTNERSHIPS

Going from Good-2-Great

We initiated a "Going from Good-2-Great" (G2G) campaign to align the whole organization with our new management goals. All leaders were required to read *Going from Good to Great,* the bestseller by Jim Collins. Our G2G initiative focused on five communication themes: 1) our motivation for change; 2) creating a vision and framework for change; 3) developing political support for change; 4) managing the transition; and 5) sustaining our momentum of change.

"Going from Good-2-Great" became our rallying cry. We created working groups, visual posters, and even t-shirts that said "Going from Good-2-Great." This initiative motivated us to make Unity Care the best possible child-serving agency providing the highest quality services.

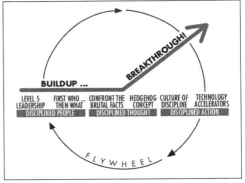

A poster we created to promote our "Going from Good-2-Great" campaign

Over the next few months we put together a plan outlining everything we needed to do to go from a good to a great organization. Sheila and I reviewed the plan with all of our staff, our oversight committee, and board of directors. To implement it, we hired some new staff members and moved a few off the bus who weren't performing up to our new standards.

At our annual Town Hall meeting on September 23, we had a lot to celebrate. We thanked God for his faithfulness and reminded ourselves of the importance of keeping our eyes on Him and not on our circumstances. We went over our history and what we had learned, so we could maximize the benefits from it.

Sheila Mitchell had already announced her desire to move on to a new opportunity as Chief Deputy Probation Officer with Los Angeles County Probation Department. As an expression of our appreciation for her dedicated service, I gave her a miniature statue of an eagle. "In the Bible, an eagle is the symbol of new and higher possibilities," I told her. "You've been like an eagle to us. You have helped raise Unity Care to a whole new level, and I am confident God has wonderful plans for you."

From left: Mark Yolton, vice president of the Unity Care board of directors, Sheila Mitchell with her eagle award, the author, and Carl Agers, chairman of the board.

I then addressed the entire staff: "God has His hand on this organization. This isn't about you or me. It's about our doing the great work that He is allowing us to do."

After the meeting, I pulled Sheila aside. "You were about to start a prestigious job in Albemarle County, Virginia. You sacrificed that security to come to work at Unity Care at a time when we were facing big challenges. What caused you to make that decision?"

"André, you were the first person from the non-profit community to welcome me when I became the head probation officer for Santa Clara County in 2004, and our friendship deepened during the twelve years we worked together. I have the greatest admiration for you and Unity Care, and I wanted to do everything I could to make sure kids and families continued to benefit from the fine work you are doing."

CHAPTER 15

EXPANDING OUR FOOTPRINT

In 2014, the Unity Care board and executive staff developed a five-year strategic plan to guide our priorities from 2015 to 2020. One of the key aspects of this plan was our "3G" initiative. It was to be a roadmap for expanding Unity Care's impact across our entire service continuum. But because of the organizational chaos that ensued immediately after we developed the plan, we were forced to put it on the back burner. Now that we were hitting the reset button, we decided to refocus our attention on this vital initiative.

The 3Gs stood for *Gaps, Growth*, and *Geography*. As part of the initiative, we identified gaps in our services that impacted our ability to effectively meet all of the needs of the youths and families we served. Then, we identified how we needed to grow our capabilities, so our staff would have all the tools and other resources they needed to fill the service gaps we had identified. Finally, we determined how we should expand our geographical footprint, so every office/community where Unity Care provided services would have access to the same resources and capabilities as clients in our home county of Santa Clara.

As we conducted our analysis, we realized that the largest gap in our services was the lack of housing for current and former foster youths. This need was a major reason why I had started Unity Care some twenty-five years before. Even then, one of my primary goals was to ensure that every young person had a safe place to live with caring adults providing unconditional care. Unfortunately, that's typically not the case, and countless numbers of youths in foster care become homeless. As I related in Chapter 6 through the story of Carl, that can sometimes tragically end in death.

The Worsening Crisis of Homelessness

Across the United States today, more than 30 percent of youths and adults age eighteen to thirty-four live with a parent. That's an increase of more than 30 percent since the year 2000. In California, the percentage of youths in this age group living at home is at least 34 percent. That's 4 percent above the national average and an increase of 36 percent since 2000.[18]

[18] These figures, which are based on 2013 data, are almost certainly higher today. For more information, see https://siliconvalleyindicators.org/data/place/housing/multigenerational-households-2/young-adults-living-with-a-parent-1980-2013/

Why do so many young adults today choose to live with one or more parent, and why is California above the national average? Unfortunately, the driving force behind these statistics is not improved parent-child relationships; it's the high cost of housing. Young adults are finding it increasingly difficult to survive financially on their own, so they must live with one or more parents. The especially high percentage of youths living at home in California is due to the higher than average costs of housing in this state.

This begs the question, if so many youths must live with their families, what's happening to youths who have no stable families? The answer is that a great many of them become homeless.

The San Francisco Bay Area has one of the largest and least sheltered homeless populations in the country. Although this region is one of the most prosperous in the world, every night thousands of people sleep on our streets. A recently published report in the *San Jose Mercury News* stated that a $216,181 household income is needed to buy a median-priced home in the San Jose metropolitan area. That was the highest income requirement among the nation's metros, according to a study by the HSH.com mortgage information website.[19]

The Bay Area is facing a crisis of epic proportions, and the situation could be about to get worse — much worse! The Continuum of Care Reform initiative recently enacted by the state legislature with good intentions may, at least in the short term, create significant problems.

Continuum of Care Reform (Assembly Bill 403)

California's Continuum of Care Reform (CCR-AB403) is a herculean effort to move thousands of youths from group homes to family-based services. Under the new system, group homes, such as the ones provided by Unity Care, will be converted into short-term residential treatment programs (STRTPs), where youths will receive high-quality mental health treatment services over a six-month period, with the goal of ultimately transitioning these youths to more permanent, stable environments with family or approved foster homes.[20]

I commend the states leadership as this reform is a bold effort at fixing the system. I believe this reform is an encouraging trend. It's a needed push to get kids into permanent homes. As I have said, the overarching goal of foster care should be to reconnect youths with responsible family members, and if that's not feasible, to place them in homes with families who can offer them stable, permanent care.

Unfortunately, no one could have seen or predicted the complexity of this task and the time and resources needed. As a result, it appears that this new initiative,

[19] https://www.mercurynews.com/2018/01/19/bay-area-housing-and-you-thought-you-were-already-depressed/
[20] For more about the CCR issue, see https://chronicleofsocialchange.org/blogger-co-op/californias-continuum-care-reform-will-produce-promised

which in theory is needed to shift the system, may in practice create huge challenges during its rollout. The state's foster care system is considerably behind the curve in finding foster and adoptive homes to take the youths who are being turned out of group homes. There are approximately 62,000 youths in the state's foster care system, with about 5,000 in group homes. As this transition from group homes to STRTPs goes into effect, it's possible that the number of foster and adoptive homes will fall far short of the need. Ultimately, a great many youths could end up on the street.

To compound the challenges, in an attempt to raise the standards of care, the process has become extremely cumbersome for group homes to qualify as STRTPs. Unity Care was the sixth organization in the state to meet the new regulatory requirements of CCR and become a STRTP, but a great many smaller residential facilities, even though they may provide high quality care, will not be able to afford the time and expense to qualify. Many of these smaller homes are operated by people of color, and it's a shame to lose them, because they best match the demographics of the foster youth population they serve.

CCR is designed to better serve the highest needs foster youth with extreme traumas and significant mental health challenges. Raising the standards of care with timely and culturally appropriate mental health services is well overdue. In order for this effort to succeed, the state, counties, communities, and foster care providers will need to increase their level of shared intent and collaboration. This effort will require increased amount of time, resources, and commitment, as well as a new way of thinking.

As part of our refocusing efforts, Unity Care's board of directors and executive team intensively discussed this ever-deepening crisis of homelessness for youths aging out of foster care. After much study and deliberation, we made an aggressive commitment to increase our housing capacity and focus more attention on finding families. We determined that these were the two most important things we could do to ensure that youths who leave our care do not end up on the streets.

As I mentioned in Chapter 7, family finding is about finding one or more members of a foster child's immediate or extended family who are capable of caring for the child, and then connecting this family member with the child. Unity Care leadership decided to prioritize finding families, because we believe an increased emphasis on finding families is one of the best ways to improve the welfare of the children in foster care and the efficacy of the system as a whole.

Realizing that our commitment to providing safe, affordable, and stable housing for all youths leaving our care without a family placement would require a substantial increase in housing capacity, and that this increase in capacity would require a great deal of money, Unity Care's board and executive team decided to launch a major gifts campaign at our annual YouthLive! gala in August 2018, with the goal of raising $13 million by 2022.

Scaling and Expanding Project Safe Haven

For more than two decades, Unity Care has offered a continuum of housing options that parallels the experiences of youth in non-foster-care situations. For example, most youths who grow up with their natural parents and leave home to go to college initially live in a dorm. As they mature, they may move out to share housing with several classmates, sometimes in a fraternity or sorority house. After that, they may move into an apartment, either alone or with one or two friends.

In a similar manner, Unity Care has arranged for dorm-style apartments, shared homes, and individual apartment units in the community. We've also partnered with developers who have created carve-outs in their housing communities, which they offer at reduced rents to youths aging out of foster care. In the Bay Area, for example, MidPen Housing, one of the state's largest providers of affordable housing, has set aside several subsidized units for former foster youths, so they can have a secure home while attending school and working.

This is a win-win-win proposition. The youths get safe, affordable apartments; the community gets productive, tax-contributing young adults; and the developer gets considerable good will and an opportunity to contribute to the community. In fact, this arrangement is producing such phenomenal results that we are planning to replicate it elsewhere.

Our overall housing initiative, which we've named Project Safe Haven, will allow us to scale our existing housing continuum into communities where housing for youths aging out of foster care is a critical need. For some time, we've been providing 150 homes in Santa Clara County, and Unity Care's recent acquisition of MAC's Children & Family Services, a non-profit agency in the San Francisco area, has added a ten-unit apartment complex and several shared homes to our housing capacity.

Project Safe Haven is a proven concept that works! The needs are great, and we intend to continue to grow organically and by acquisitions to meet them.

Replicating Imani Village

Meanwhile, Unity Care continues to pioneer new approaches in education. Now that we have successfully tested the Imani Village initiative highlighted in Chapter 12, we are preparing to introduce it in other parts of Northern California.

Senator Dianne Feinstein, Senator Barbara Boxer, and Congresswoman Zoe Lofgren have all expressed enthusiasm about Imani Village[21]. Congresswoman Lofgren and members of the staffs of Senators Boxer and Feinstein have visited school sites where Imani Village is installed. They have been impressed and encouraged by the enthusiastic praise of school superintendents, principals, administrators, counselors, and teachers.

I believe Imani Village has the potential to dramatically transform the way

[21] These lawmakers and others have enthusiastically endorsed Project Safe Haven as well.

we educate kids who live in underserved communities and attend low-performing schools. I would ultimately like to see the approach replicated across the nation. The challenge will be to get educators and mental health professionals to work collaboratively and focus on engaging the community.

By and large, professionals in these two fields have different backgrounds, outlooks, and priorities. They get their funding from different sources, and they measure their results in different ways. It's going to be a long-term battle to get them to come out of their silos and address the issue of education holistically. But I'm excited about fighting this battle, because the lives of millions of kids across our nation are at stake.

25@YouthLive!

At our annual gala on August 25, 2018, Unity Care celebrated its twenty-fifth birthday! Our keynote speaker for "25@YouthLive!" was educator, author, and businessman Stedman Graham. Joelle Williams, a recent Stanford graduate, was our amazing youth speaker.

That evening, we also honored Silicon Valley pioneer Roy Clay, Sr. as our community champion awardee. As I mentioned, our goal is to raise $13 million by 2022 for critically needed housing for youths transitioning out of foster care. Philanthropist and community leader Linda L. Lester, winner of last year's Community Champion Award and, Darlene Woodson, adoptive parent and philanthropist, are our presenting sponsors for this year's celebration.

In some ways, it seems like only yesterday when we accepted the very first foster youth into our care on August 14, 1993. Due to the support of many and the faithfulness of God, we have been able to stay the course, survive the storms, and touch countless lives. It's been an exhilarating,

From left to right, Linda L. Lester, Breeaunna Lynn, and the author at Unity Care's YouthLive! gala in May 2017. Linda was honored with our Community Champion Award for her inspirational philanthropic endeavors, and Breeaunna was our poised and courageous keynote speaker at the event.

challenging, and rewarding journey from a single foster home with five boys to an organization with more than two hundred employees and a $17 million budget, which annually serves more than 7,500 youths and families across Northern California. I'm excited to see what's around the bend!

CHAPTER 16

A CALL TO ACTION

In this book, I've talked about many of the challenges I've seen over my twenty-five years of working with our foster care system, and I've suggested some ideas for addressing them. Here is a summary of some of my major recommendations.

- **Reduce the number of families the entering foster care system by offering more intervention and prevention services to strengthen families.** Special emphasis should be placed on reducing the disproportionality of children of color entering the system.

- **Restrict the use of the term "general neglect" to serious issues, such as the safety of children and families**. Because issues relating to well-being/poverty currently are lumped within the same "general neglect" category, millions of children across America, especially children of color, are inappropriately bouncing around in the foster care system.

- **Place more emphasis on reconnecting foster children with natural family members.** When there is substantial abuse and neglect, it certainly is necessary and appropriate to remove children from their homes. But the emphasis should be on finding other members of the family — uncles, aunts, grandparents, cousins, or other capable relatives — who would be willing to open their homes. If an appropriate family member cannot be found, the child should be placed in a foster home or adoptive home.

- **Promote greater trust between families and communities with needs and the human service agencies and non-profit providers who serve them.** One way to enhance trust is through better understanding of the historical, multi-dimensional dynamics that have shaped the values and traditions of these communities.

- **Provide training to all service providers and child welfare professionals to promote cultural proficiency.** Emphasis should be on viewing all domains of life from a healing-centered perspective that focuses on people's potential, instead of from a deficit-based perspective that focuses on their deficiencies. All professionals and organizations providing services should intentionally seek to discard prior assumptions and engage in all discussions, treatment decisions, and other interactions with good will.

- **Devote the same level of intent, resources, and support to engaging the fathers as is currently devoted to engaging the mothers.** Too often, the foster care system focuses only on supporting the mother, while the father is listed as "unknown." This may indicate a systemic bias against males.

- **Ensure that all social workers and other human services professionals understand how traumas impact the attitudes and behaviors of individuals, families, and communities.** Because social workers have so much power over the people they serve, they should understand how their own actions can unconsciously create trauma in the lives of the families they are serving. Even asking a family to come in for a meeting can create trauma.

- **Focus more attention on finding families for youths aging out of foster care and providing housing for them, so they do not end up on the streets.** Homelessness among former foster care youths is a serious problem that is rapidly worsening.

- **Incorporate the spiritual dimension into the child welfare system.** People are often reluctant to talk about the issue of spirituality, but it undergirds every culture. Social service agencies should be allowed to incorporate the spiritual dimension into their work. Child welfare organizations are better able to engage with and serve minority families and communities when they establish working relationships with faith-based organizations.

- **Create a customer service culture within the child welfare system that puts people first.** Much can be learned from studying and imitating private-sector companies who are recognized for their outstanding customer service. For example, most successful for-profit companies regularly solicit feedback from their customers. Organizations providing social services could institute similar feedback systems, so individuals and families receiving services can comment on their quality.

- **Encourage federal and state legislatures to give states and counties more flexibility in spending.** The Title IV-E Waiver program in foster care, which allows government institutions to direct more funds toward prevention and early intervention, is one positive example of such legislation.

- **Measure outcomes instead of outputs, so government and non-profit organizations that provide services will focus on results instead of**

merely on activities. Tracking outcomes promotes and measures progress. More often than not, tracking outputs simply increases the administrative burden.

- **Encourage government agencies to become agencies of healing that display a welcoming attitude.** Their priority should be to empower the people they serve, not to exercise power over them. Their goal should be to value, honor, and respect their clients, not to marginalize them. Holding their clients accountable is important, but serving their clients well, especially by helping them deal with trauma, is even more important.

- **Create educational models that provide culturally proficient integrated mental health and academic supports in collaboration with the local communities and schools.** Our Imani Village initiative has successfully demonstrated how youths and communities benefit when schools, county systems, and communities step out of their silos and work holistically.

Growing Roses in Concrete

There's an African proverb which says, "It takes a village to raise a child." That has certainly been true with Unity Care. I am overwhelmed with gratitude for all the dedicated individuals, government agencies, and other organizations that have invested their time, talents, and treasure toward our success. These include our home county of Santa Clara and the other fine counties in which we operate, our community of supporters, our volunteers, our staff members, our board members, and our service partners.

I also am overwhelmed with thankfulness to God for giving us the enormous privilege of offering hope and inspiration to thousands of our society's most vulnerable children, youth, and families. Over the years, He has faithfully provided for our needs, sometimes miraculously, and we give Him all the glory for whatever success we have had.

My twenty-five years at Unity Care have been filled with tremendous joy. There also have been plenty of heartaches and trials. I wouldn't want to repeat the trials, but I can honestly say that I am thankful for them. Unity Care as an organization, including all of us who have weathered these storms, are stronger as a result. I often recall our 2015 YouthLive! gala, when Elizabeth Cartagena, a graduate of our program, passionately challenged the other foster care graduates in attendance with the following words:

> *"Just know that we are gold. We've been through the fire...This life is preparing you for great things, but you have to go through the fire to get there."*

Elizabeth's words are marvelously relevant to you and me. We are made for great things, and we must go through the fire to get there. Fire, though painful, purifies our motives, gives birth to new vision, and refines our plans. When we are willing to step out of our comfort zones and passionately pursue the plans God has for us, He grants us the joy of participating with Him in bringing hope to the hopeless and growing roses in concrete.

ABOUT THE AUTHOR

André Chapman, founder and CEO of The Unity Care Group, entered non-profit work after a successful career in high-tech sales. He earned his Bachelor of Science in Business from San Jose State in 1988, his Masters in Organization Management from the University of Phoenix in 2001, and a Certificate of Completion in Strategic Perspectives on Non-Profit Management from Harvard Business School in 2004.

Mr. Chapman has received numerous awards for his dedicated service to youth and his community, including the following:

- "Grand Hero" award, presented by Bob Dole and the Avanti Foundation at the Magic Ceremony

- "Partner of the Decade" award, presented by the City of San Jose Department of Housing

- "Nonprofit of the Year" award, presented by 100 Black Men of Silicon Valley

- "Evelyn T. Robinson Outstanding African American Alumnus" award, presented by San Jose State University

- "Recognition for Outstanding & Invaluable Services to the Community," presented by Congresswoman Zoe Lofgren and Congressman Mike Honda

- "Joe Perry & Wally Yonamine Unity Award," presented by the San Francisco 49ers

André and Teresa Chapman and family today. Front row (left to right): Christiana Arriola, Teresa Chapman, the author, Ariana Chapman. Back row: Ronnie Arriola, Aaron Chapman, Renee Arriola, and Andre' Chapman, Jr.

ABOUT UNITY CARE

Unity Care Group, Inc. is a strength-based, family-focused, culturally profi-cient youth and family development agency. Its mission is to "provide quality youth and family programs for the purpose of creating healthier communities through lifelong partnerships." Over the past twenty-five years, Unity Care has developed the organizational capacity, community recognition, and financial strength to effectively deliver supportive welfare, mental health, and juvenile justice services to more than 7,500 youths and families every year.

Unity Care has a multiculturally diverse staff of 200 employees and an an-nual budget of $17 million. It serves communities that are approximately 38 per-cent Latino, 28 percent African American, 25 percent Caucasian, and 9 percent Asian/Pacific Islander.

Unity Care's Board of Directors, from left to right: Mark Yolton, Carl Agers, Elizabeth Pappy, the author, Madison Le, David Hershfield, Marty Cull, and Cedric Martin. Not pictured: Ray Ruiz, Anita Lynch, and James Park

Unity Care
1400 Parkmoor Ave, Suite 115, San Jose, CA 95126
408-510-3480
www.unitycare.org

CPSIA information can be obtained
at www.ICGtesting.com
Printed in the USA
FSHW02n0442130818
51303FS